Corsets

A Modern Guide

Corsets

A Modern Guide

Velda Lauder

CHARTWELL
BOOKS, INC.

A Quantum Book

This edition published in 2010 by
CHARTWELL BOOKS, INC.
A division of BOOK SALES, INC.
276 Fifth Avenue, Suite 206
New York, New York 10001
USA

ISBN 13: 978-0-7858-2671-2
ISBN 10: 0-7858-2671-8

QUMCAMG

This book is produced by
Quantum Publishing Ltd
6 Blundell Street
London N7 9BH

Project Editor: Samantha Warrington
Editorial Assistant: Jo Morley
Designer: Andrew Easton
Production: Rohana Yusof
Publisher: Sarah Bloxham

Printed in Singapore by
Star Standard Industries (Pte) Ltd.

Cover image: Velda Lauder 'Celtic Swirl' corset, 2009. © Gregory Michael King,
model Dominique de Merteuil.

Table of Contents

Introduction   9

History of the Corset   27

Modern Corset Culture   83

The Corset as Fetish object   117

The Corset as High Fashion   143

Variations on the Classic Corset   171

The Modern Girl's guide to Corset Wearing   197

Index   220

Bibliography   222
Picture Credits   224

Written by: Velda Lauder
Additional research: Jill Thompson
Dedicated to: Michael Garrod

Special Thanks to:
Bobette, Regis Hertrich, Rod Howe, James & James, Gregory Michael King, Koneko, Ariel B
Majtas, Maria Thompson, Charlet, Morrigan Hel, Fiona Jade, Deanne Lula Lee, Viktoria Modesta,
Bex Paul, Maz Spencer, Elaine Tang.

About the Author

A graduate of the College of Marketing & Design in Dublin, Ireland, Velda Lauder cut her teeth in the fashion coordination and display team at the department store of Brown Thomas & Company. After winning a prestigious Smirnoff Young Designer of the Year Award, Velda joined the creative design team for premiere Ibiza nightclub, Ku. Relocating to London in 1996, she worked as a stylist for Tatler *and* Opera Now *while designing clothing for rock stars and royalty. Her first U.K. collection, "Warrior Woman", was featured at London Fashion Week with Wayne Hemmingway's Red or Dead label. Her design company and Soho-based store, Pagan Metal, provided the platform to launch her groundbreaking corset collection "Vanity" in 1997, employing for the first time her unique Uber-Curve method of corset construction and tailoring. Velda Lauder has designed for the Coco De Mer Couture Collection, been commissioned for one-off pieces by Karl Lagerfeld, Victoria's Secret annual TV shows, Dita Von Teese, Courtney Love, promo videos for George Michael's "An Easier Affair" and Robbie Williams' "Love Light", plus stage costumes for Pete Burns, Sarah Brightman and numerous burlesque stars including Miss Lily White and Miss Polly Rae.*

Cut out of Marilyn Monroe wearing a corset in Seligman, Arizona, on "Historic Route 66" USA.

Introduction

This book traces the development of the corset from ancient to modern times, paying particular attention to its popular resurgence as an outer garment from the late 20th century to the present day. The author, Velda Lauder, is one of the most celebrated corset designers of our times. Here, she combines extensive reference material alongside a personal journey through the evolution of the corset. Velda's enthusiasm and fascination with her subject make her ideally qualified to write about the corset from the viewpoint of an industry insider who has devoted the last 15 years to celebrating the female form through tailoring and corsetry techniques. This is her journey in her own words ...

LIKE MANY OTHERS, I first became fascinated with the corset on rainy afternoons watching classic black-and-white movies as a child. The iconic screen goddess with her delicious curves, tiny waist, and heaving bosom made a huge visual impression on my young mind. The magnetic power of Marilyn Monroe as she wiggled her voluptuous magnificence across the screen, while possessing a 20-inch corseted waist, was unforgettable. Television and movie images of both familiar screen idols and anonymous showgirls tightening their corsets caught my imagination and my Barbie's homemade wardrobe was forever changing.

The timeless and enduring beauty of the corset is at once ancient and futuristic. It evokes the legendary female warrior in her armored bodice, but in the present day is increasingly fused with images of modern comic-book heroines. A controversial garment constantly evolving yet always classic, full of paradoxes, the corset is both underwear and outerwear, a symbol of chastity and restraint while at the same time highly erotic. Does it subjugate women or empower them? Is it titillation or armor? Is it made to conceal or reveal the body?

Warrior queens

Tightlacing, constraint, and corsetry – practices and garments that have the power to change the shape of the body – have been around since humans first began to clothe themselves. They were just one part of a

Lady unfastening corset, 19th century.

tradition that used clothing as a form of tribal recognition and a way of defining one's tribal allegiance and individuality.

Some of the earliest visual evidence comes from a series of Neolithic drawings from Norfolk, in the east of England, that depict women wearing front-laced animal-hide bodices. Statues of the Cretan snake goddess dating from 1500 BCE show her dressed in a shapely bodice while wielding snakes in both hands. Boudicca or Boadicea, queen of the Iceni, and the Celtic warrior queen Maeve of Ireland are both depicted in ancient art and legend as wearing leather bodices as part of their battle armor – a garment of both empowerment and protection.

The changing shape of fashion

Over hundreds of years, the bodice, which was initially simply a waist cincher and support, evolved into the more complex boned garment known as the corset. Early bodices relied on the strength of their fabric to give support and tension. The more sophisticated corset could be produced from comparatively softer fabrics, using boning to provide the shape and structure. The popularity of the corset began to take off in Renaissance Venice, where ladies of fashion, aided by heavy boning within their garments, strived for a straight conical torso, high neckline, and flat chest. The 18th and 19th centuries saw the boned corset reach the height of its popularity, but it went into decline in the early 20th century.

The emancipation that followed World War One led women to seek a release from boning and restriction, and structured corsets became unpopular, replaced by less restrictive cording and quilting. In the 1920s, increased sexual freedom and the boyish flapper look further diminished interest in the corset, until the elasticated girdles of the 1930s finally eliminated the traditional corset as an everyday garment forever.

Modern resurgence

In the last 25 years, there has been a revival in interest in traditional corsets, probably inspired by the influential designer Vivienne Westwood, who first came to prominence as part of the punk movement. Renowned for her interest in form and structure, and drawing inspiration from the past, Westwood included the "Statue of Liberty" corset, explicitly designed to be worn as outer clothing, as part of her 1987 "Harris Tweed" Collection. Indeed, Westwood and punk introduced fetish garments to the world of fashion and paved the way for overtly sexual clothing and fetishistic garments to be gradually integrated into the mainstream.

In more recent times every major fashion house has dabbled with the corset. The couture catwalks frequently responding to its siren call. From Christian Dior and Christian Lacroix to Jean Paul Gaultier and Alexander McQueen, satins, silks, leather, rubber, plastic, chrome and even wood have been used to craft the modern couture corset.

Models on the catwalk wearing corsets as outerwear, Vivienne Westwood sping/summer collection, 1990.

Fiona Jade in "Goddess" pose, Velda Lauder "Polka-dot and Pinstripe" collection, 2005.

Corset inspirations

Body modification is present in most cultures, contemporary and archaic, western and global. The tightly bound golden lotus feet to which Chinese women aspired in the 13th to 20th centuries is one of the most extreme examples, as are the brass neck rings of the Penaung women of Burma, another highly visual illustration of the human quest for transformation and reconstruction.

The Dinka people of Sudan in East Africa wear elaborate beaded waist and neck corsets to indicate their status and wealth. For his 1997 Christian Dior couture collection, John Galliano drew inspiration from the Dinka corset culture with stunning effect.

The power of the corset

The corset has been a controversial garment throughout its history. It has been seen as a means of female oppression and yet sexual empowerment, of class distinction and yet a conduit of power. This remarkable garment covers the whole of the torso, sculpting the body into an hourglass-shaped work of art, accentuating the curves while diminishing the bulges. The magic of corsets is such that through the ages women, and sometimes men, have reported heightened feelings of sexual energy, personal power, and social standing when wearing one.

Charlet in polka-dot demi cup suspender corset, Velda lauder "Polka-dot and pinstripe" collection, 2005.

Fiona Jade wearing antique rose glitter "curve" corset, Velda Lauder, 2007.

Samppa Von Cyborg, Finnish-born, London-based body modification artist.

The corset has been worn by the society ladies of the high Renaissance, the respectable middle-class women of the Victorian era and that quintessentially modern icon, Madonna, one of the great exponents of the 20th-century corset. The corset gives instant, yet temporary, body modification. Support, deportment, and an elegant grace are the side effects of the upright alignment of the spine. As a consequence, corset wearers look taller and feel stronger, the "inner goddess" is freed, the internal beauty and power of a woman liberated.

Changing the body

Growing health and body consciousness in the 20th and 21st centuries has led to great interest in changing and sculpting the physique, using diet, exercise and even steroids and growth hormones for maximum musculature and definition. Pilates is an exercise system that focuses on the core postural muscles that provide support for the spine, essentially training the muscles within the torso to do the job of the corset.

Today, the corset has been joined by other body arts, including tattooing and piercing and, more recently, the surreal implants popularized by the Finnish-born, London-based Samppa von Cyborg. Extreme body arts and modification are now an accepted part of our society today, whether it is as simple as the act of dyeing one's hair, or as extreme as the surgical procedures of having a face lift or liposuction.

We may think that personal physical expression has reached its peak in our modern era, but a close study of the evidence shows that humans have always striven to reinvent themselves. Perhaps it is just that our means and methods are simply more sophisticated and varied today.

A personal corset epiphany

The potential of the corset for evolution and expression fascinated me, and one night, when a friend of mine fainted at a gig while wearing a badly-made corset, it all suddenly made sense. I released her from the offending garment and immediately began to mentally redesign its anatomy so it would fit her form more appropriately. Her corset had been made from an unmodified Victorian pattern and was putting great pressure on her ribs and lungs. 20th-century women are considerably larger than Victorian women – and a significantly different shape – so adaptation was required.

Months of research and mentoring followed as I deepened my knowledge of corset construction. Both myself and the master corsetière, Mr. Pearl, share a common mentor in "Jeannette," who introduced me to the late, great Michael Garrod, who dedicated his life to preserving the art of corsetry. Under Michael Garrod's expert tutelage, I learned the technical side of corset-making which gave me a solid foundation from which to develop my own unique style, patterns and cutting methods.

What I seek in a well-cut modern corset is the ability to shape and sculpt the waist without crushing a woman's ribs or hips, so freeing her inner goddess. Whoever wears the corset should be transformed by it in what is truly a "red carpet moment," a wondrous couture experience.

The corset symbolizes the divine, demonic, and desirable, and elicits controversy and sensation wherever it is shown. My own obsession with the corset as my canvas for expression has lasted for over 15 years and has been a constant source of inspiration and creativity as I continue to discover new and fascinating aspects of this unique garment.

Velda Lauder, June 2010

Model Laura Beduz
wearing Velda Lauder
"Polka-dot and pinstripe"
collection, 2005.

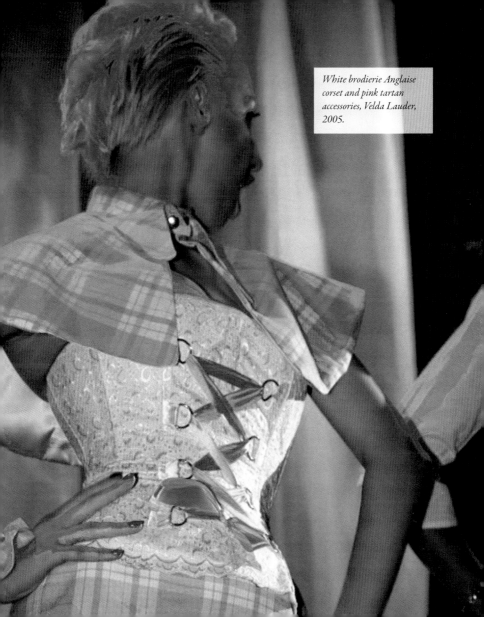

Thomson's company trade card illustration of their patent glove fitting corsets, circa 1880.

History of the Corset

Throughout history, humans have used different means to change their appearance. The corset is one of the most significant and enduring. Over time, it has evolved from the armored bodice worn by ancient goddesses and warrior queens to a means of dramatically changing and shaping the female body. The changing shape and function of the corset have reflected both fashion and the fluctuating role of women in society. While women in the past used the corset to shape their bodies to fit their clothes, today's devotees often use it as outerwear and it has become a proud part of the 21st-century woman's everyday wardrobe.

DURING ITS HISTORY, the corset has changed radically in shape and function. Medieval women wore pairs of bodices strengthened with wood or bone in order to encase and flatten the curves of the body. From the 16th century through to the 18th century the desired shape of the torso was conical, tapering to a small waist. By the 19th century, following a brief return to a more natural shape when the empire line was in fashion, the corset took on an hourglass shape that emphasized the hips and bust. The 20th century saw advances in fabric technology used to make the corset more wearable and comfortable, although it was swiftly overtaken by the introduction of the bra and girdle.

Women's underwear has had a variety of functions throughout history. It protected the skin from the rough fabrics of the outer clothing and shielded the outer fabrics from what was often a long-unwashed body beneath. This was essential at a time when the fabrics from which outer garments were made were often very difficult to wash and personal hygiene was limited. In the chilly British climate undergarments were essential throughout the year as protection against the elements.

Corsets in ancient times

Lacing and corsetry have been employed in one form or another since humans began to clothe themselves. Neolithic drawings from Britain depict women wearing front-laced, animalhide bodices. In western civilization, the corset evolved from the waist-cinching support provided by the front-laced bodice, but whereas the bodice relied on tough, strong fabric to give support, the corset used boning for its structure and form.

Before the invention of the button in the middle of the 17th century, lacing with various types of cord and ribbon would have been the most effective way of closing garments securely. As a result, lacing and tightening have been associated with warmth, security, decoration, and tribal identity. Different tribes employed distinctive methods of lacing and tying, the variations distinguishing the culture of one ethnic group from another. The basis of many cultural traditions and much folk art have their roots in the daily chores associated with food, clothing, and shelter, and the methods humans used to dress have had a profound an effect on culture in general.

Symbol of empowerment

In tracing the development of the corset through the ages, it is important to examine the role that women have held in society from ancient times. In western Europe and the Middle East early female deities were often worshiped as the creator goddess and the giver of all life. It may have been that the position of women in these societies was politically on a similar or even an elevated footing to that of men. Certainly priestesses,

Boudicca (or Boadicea), Queen of Celtic tribe the Iceni, 1st century BCE. Leader of the uprising of tribes against the occupying forces of the Roman Empire. Original illustration by R. E Groves, 1907.

queens, and female warriors were well-established figures in oral history. In ancient times, corsets were a symbol of female empowerment, and ancient art shows godesses, queens and priestesses wearing them. Some of the earliest examples include statues dating from 1500 BCE that show the bodice-wearing Cretan snake goddess wielding snakes in both hands. Boudicca (Boadicea) and the Celtic warrior Queen Maeve wore leather bodices as an essential part of their battle armour.

However, over time, women took less and less part in the waging of war and the female warrior fell out of favour. Historians have suggested that the value placed on a woman's reproductive abilities meant that it was too risky to allow young fertile women to take up arms and fight for their tribes. This may have led to women's exclusion from tribal decision-making processes and a subsequent reduction in their overall power.

From protection to subjugation

Around 5,000 years ago, a new religion established by the prophet Abraham began to rise to prominence. The first book of the Old Testament, the book of Genesis, contains the story of the descent of Adam and Eve from the Garden of Eden. In the tale, Eve is depicted as collaborating with the serpent and leading Adam to disobey God's command not to eat from the tree of knowledge. As a result, Eve has often been portrayed as responsible for humankind's banishment from the garden.

From the time of the rise of the monotheistic religions, the creation story has reinforced the marginalization and mistrust of women. Over the last 5,000 years, in most societies women have been disenfranchized and discriminated against in every area of social and political interaction. Not until the 20th century were most western women able to take part in the political process and vote for a government of their choice.

Controlling the female body

The female silhouette tends to evolve as a result of what is considered socially acceptable and desirable at any given time. Throughout history women have worn the most elaborate contraptions, involving strapping, binding, boning, and lacing, in order to achieve the perfect, fashionable shape for the bust, hips and buttocks.

In the 21st century we tend to think of lingerie as floating delicately over the skin, a bra perhaps enhancing the bust with some padded underwiring which lifts and separates, but ultimately consisting of a sensual and comfortable collection of undergarments. However the history of the purpose of lingerie, and particularly the corset, has been one of control and constraint; clothing worn for the express purpose of arranging and manipulating the natural female form into something that was both pleasing to the eye and conformed to the norms of society and the fashions of the time.

Although the corset may have at one time been seen as a symbol of women's subjugation and submission, by the early 21st century, however, the corset has come to symbolize power and strength for many women who wear them.

Fashion and female status

Fashion and trends in womenswear over the ages have often been driven by society's perception of women; either in the suppression or the celebration of her curvaceous fecundity. In Medieval times, women had limited legal status and few rights; they were considered first the property of their fathers, and then the property of their husbands. They were rarely educated, could not own property and had limited possibilities for employment. In religion and folklore, women were often portrayed as temptresses who corrupted men and whose original sin had paved the way for the fall of man from God's grace.

Without a husband a woman had little status, and many unmarried women were persecuted and some executed as witches. Female children were married as soon as a husband and suitable dowry could be found. With no legal age for marriage, girls as young as 12 were often married to older men. Complications in childbirth frequently resulted in stillborn children or the death of the mother; the average life expectancy for medieval women was only 30 years.

Charlemagne and courtiers,
8th century. The women
wear broad corset-like
belts and girdles amd long
braided hair.

Misconceptions about undergarments

At a time when undergarments were rarely if ever on view, the curiosity of the medieval male as to the exact nature of the underclothing worn by women resulted in some very far-fetched imaginings which may have distorted historical understanding of the development of the corset.

C. Willett and P. Cunnington commented, in *The History of Underclothes,* that, "A good deal of masculine scorn was provoked by [the under-bodices]." They quote Philip Gosson who stated that "These privie coats by art made strong / With bones and steels and suchlike ware / Whereby their back and sides grow long / And now they harnest gallants are / Were they for use against the foe / Our dames for amazons might go!" Willett and Cunnington go on to say, "There are occasional references to "iron bodies" and specimens of these, resembling armour and perforated with holes, exist in museums. These, however, are now regarded as orthopaedic instruments, when they are not – as is commonly the case – fanciful "reproductions." There is no evidence that they were worn by women as stays."

Compressing the bust

In the Middle Ages, women's undergarments were used less as a protection and more to change the shape of the body to meet a prevailing ideal perhaps of subservient womanhood. Medieval undergarments flattened breasts and curves, leading to a more childlike outline.

Throughout the period, the breasts were hidden and flattened with controlling bodices, corsetry and binding to make the bust appear compressed and small. A woman's underclothes were rarely visible and were frequently designed to disguise her natural female form. Certainly, with the breasts flattened and the waistline hidden within the conical-shaped bodice of a dress, it would have been difficult to imagine that there were curves secreted beneath.

Fabrics used for underclothes would have been soft and relatively expensive linen or even silk for the upper classes and hemp or woollen materials for poorer people. Women wore a full-length, usually long-sleeved, smock or chemise as an undergarment. Tight bandaging around the waist or some form of stays may have been employed to give form to the outer dress. The underbodices of this time were frequently known as a "bodies" or a "pair of bodies" as they were made of two parts, and strengthened with wood or whalebone.

Anne of Denmark (1574 –1619), married to James I of England in 1589. Depicted wearing a dress in the Renaissance fashion of a conical bodice and farthingale to hold out the skirt.

Conical corsets

The Renaissance was a period of padding, pulling, and pushing into yet more extreme cone-shaped bodices with tiny low waists. From the late 14th century to the early 16th century, wealthier women wore gowns made from a range of exotic fabrics layered one on top of another and with a huge amount of padding underneath. The bodices and corsets of the time were worn with petticoats or farthingales that held out the skirts in a firm conical shape. The tightlacing, which required the services of a maid to enable a woman to dress, resulted in the most impractical of clothing, and an upright posture, but the inability to bend at the waist.

By the 16th century, women were wearing corsets and clothing that appeared deliberately designed to hide away the natural form, with the breasts completely flattened and the curve from the waist to the bosom disguised within an inverted conical shape. As well as the more expensive whalebone, bone and even wood would have been used to stiffen the corset, which would not have allowed for much flexibility and was almost certainly uncomfortable for the wearer.

These garments were designed to encourage the torso into the then fashionable cylindrical outline, whilst flattening and elevating the bust. This use of corsetry signals a shift in the concept of tailoring, moving away clothing that was designed to bind and support the existing body shape, as had been the case during the early Renaissance period, corsetry was now used to encourage the body to conform to the fashionable female shape of the period.

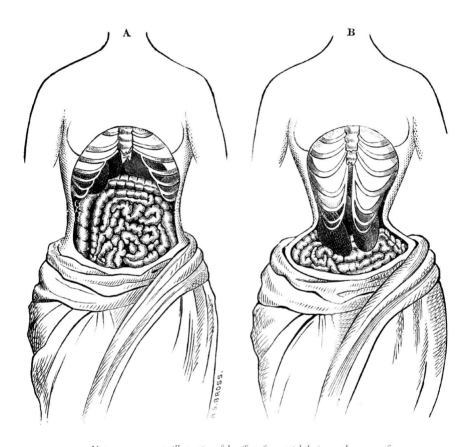

Nature versus corsets: illustration of the effect of corset tightlacing on the organs of the body. A shows the natural position of internal organs. B shows when deformd by tightlacing. In this way the liver and the stomach have been forced downward, as seen in the cut. From "Physiology for young people adapted to intermediate classes and common schools".

A fashion for the wealthy

The fashion for garments that greatly restricted movement was the preserve of royalty and the nobility. The wealthy wore ornate clothing, heavily embroidered with gold or silver thread, incorporating pearls and beads and using expensive fabrics to display their wealth and status. The clothing of the ruling class was not only a visual sign of the owner's prosperity but could also be an investment. Fabrics from overseas, such as Chinese silk and Egyptian cotton, were so valuable that garments made from these materials were frequently resold.

The working classes wore cheaper, less formal, and less restrictive clothing which allowed them to perform physical work, but even the poorest women would have worn a plain boned bodice for everyday wear.

Extreme lacing: a risk to health?

The fashion for extreme tightlacing gave rise to the phenomenon whereby well-to-do ladies were renowned for swooning and fainting because their restrictive corsets compressed the ribcage and left them breathless and incapacitated. Doctors and politicians cursed the foolishness of the this vain and absurd craze suggesting women were putting their health, even their lives, at risk. Despite this censure, the corset survived; the brassière was not to be invented until the 20th century, so women really had very few options available to keep their bosoms and waistlines in check.

"The Goodbye," copper engraving depicting 18th-century ladies' fashion, the great petticoat. Nicholas De Launay after Jean Michel Moreaeu le Jeaune, "Les adieux," circa 1775.

An inconvenient fashion

The ever-expanding farthingale provoked considerable protest and remonstration in periodicals of the time:

"Mr. Guardian – your predecessor, The Spectator, endeavored, but in vain, to improve the charms of the fair sex by exposing their dress whenever it launched into extremities. Amongst the rest the great petticoat came under his consideration, but in contradiction to whatever he has said, they still resolutely persist in this fashion. The form of their bottom is not, I confess, all together the same, for whereas before it was one of an orbicular make, they now look as if they were pressed so that they seem to deny access to any part but the middle. Many are the inconveniences that accrue to her majesty's loving subjects from the said petticoats, as hurting men's shins, sweeping down the ware of industrious females in the street, & c. I saw a young lady fall down the other day, and, believe me, sir, she very much resembled an overturned bell without a clapper. Many other disasters I could tell you of that befall themselves as well as others by means of this unwieldy garment. I wish, Mr. Guardian, you could join with me in showing your dislike of such a monstrous fashion, and I hope, when the ladies see this, the opinion of two of wisest men in England, they will be convinced of their folly. I am, sir, your daily reader and admirer - Tom Pain"

Letter to the Guardian *22 July, 1713 in W. B. Lord* "The Corset and the Crinoline."

Silk and silver thread embroidered mantua and petticoat gown, showing an extremely wide farthingale skirt, 1745-1750.

The baroque explosion

The fashionable female silhouette of the 18th century presented a full high bosom and a completely straight back, the shoulders held back so far that they almost touched one another. This look required a rigid, compressing, and long-waisted corset with a narrow back and a wide front. Once more, physicians railed against the dangerous practice of corseting the body and the dangers that might result to the internal organs.

The height of 18th-century fashion saw an explosion of decoration, ribbons, lace, and over the top flamboyance. Magnificent hooped skirts and bustle pads gave the illusion of an enormous derrière, while the corset cinched in the waist and presented a full high bosom flowing over an immodestly low-cut cleavage. Cleavage-enhancing, low-cut gowns which displayed the breasts were sometimes so revealing that ladies used scarves along the neckline to protect their modesty.

French excess

Throughout the century, women's clothing became ever more grandiose and formidable. The hooped skirts grew larger and more elaborate, with side hoops, hip panniers, and bustle pads all designed to emphasize the small corseted waist. It was considered ultra-feminine for the wealthy woman's dress to take up three times the space of a man, with imposing hooped skirts made of brightly colored stiffened fabric, elaborately

Marie Antoinette
(1755–1793) shown in
extravagant dress and
holding a rose, from
Costumes Historiques de
la France, vol. 3.

decorated with ruffles, lace, and bows. The fashion for high-heeled shoes, huge wigs, hair pads, and hats also meant that a woman's height was raised to at least that of the average man's.

Across the Channel, in France, Louis XVI and his queen, Marie Antoinette, were on the French throne. The extravagance and excess of their court, combined with the extreme accumulation of power at the top of the regime, led to a massive popular revolt. At the end of the century, in 1789, the French Revolution swept the *ancien regime* from power. A post-revolutionary backlash against anything to do with the former governing class swept away the overblown fashions of the court and ushered in a more modern natural look that was to find favor in England during the Regency period of the early 19th century.

The empire line and natural beauty
At the end of the 18th century, fashion changed dramatically, ushering in the empire line silhouette. The high-waisted empire line, influenced by the Graeco-Roman style of flowing robes, became the very height of good taste.

The softer lines of these fashions featured more natural female shapes and used lighter fabrics, without the need for shape-giving underpinnings

Colored engraving showing evening dresses in the empire line style, typical of the fashion of the time, from Le Beau Monde, *1808.*

such as farthingales and panniers. As a result, the corset styles of the early 19th century were far less constrictive; they were designed to lightly support the figure whilst shifting the bosom upwards. Fashionable ladies were delighted with the new front-lacing corsets, which allowed them to tie the lacing themselves.

Flamboyant fashions

The high-waisted empire line style traveled across from Napoleonic France to George III's England in the late 18th century. This was the era of the dandy, Beau Brummel (who once claimed that it took him five hours to dress each day), and the romantic poet Lord Byron, of excessive gambling and extravagant parties, flamboyant fashions, powdered wigs, and make-up for the gentlemen of means, and general excess.

By the time George IV came to the throne in 1820 the "Regency" style was already firmly established. Politically, the Regency period refers to the time when the Prince Regent assumed the role of his father, George III, in matters of state during the king's bouts of mental illness from1811 until his death in 1820 however the the term has come to include George IV's reign until 1837, when Queen Victoria ascended the throne.

The flamboyant style associated with George IV continued to flourish throughout his reign and initially saw the adoption of a more romantic style of dress by the ruling classes. As this fashion swept across the country, some gothic influences started to make their mark. Elizabethan ruffs, flamboyant decoration, and padding made a comeback, and bodices became more shapely.

A changing role for the corset

Prior to the Regency era, corsets were generally designed to constrain the body from hips to bust and were worn either as underwear or as the actual bodice of a gown or dress. They were fastened with a single cord forming a zig-zag up the back and often with straps over the shoulders.

Corsets were now designed more for bust enhancement and a degree of abdominal reduction or control, without excessive waist cinching. As well as formal clothing becoming generally more comfortable to wear, corsetry was further considered to improve overall posture, since it is quite impossible to slouch when wearing a corset. Both men and women were enthusiastic wearers of the corset; indeed, King George himself famously wore a corset in later years, one designed for a 50-inch waist due to his massive girth as a result of excessive indulgence.

Corset styles had become much less constrictive than in previous eras and many women wore the new lighter "stays" in both short and long versions. The short stays can be considered the genuine forerunner to our modern underwear. Designed more for support than previous models and not generally constricting, they used stiffened fabrics, straps, and laces to lightly control the figure and shift the bosom upwards.

Less emphasis on waist cinching reflected the fashion for the "natural female form" inspired by the classical Graeco-Roman styles which were so in vogue. Women's dresses were modeled on a flowing and more forgiving Grecian-style robe, with the half-blouse or "chemisette" worn underneath by day, to cover the neck area above the bust.

For the first time, ladies could wear fashionable clothing which was not designed to be unnecessarily restrictive and impractical for performing anything other than the lightest duties. Previously, the impracticality of dress was an indication of one's position as only the leisured classes could wear clothing that restricted their movement. Although working women wore corsets, they would wear a much less restrictive "corselet" which laced up at the front and did not require a maid to fasten it.

These new softer lines, although short-lived, were totally radical; to dress without farthingales, hoops, bustles or tightly corseted waists represented a complete revolution in womenswear. The more natural silhouettes and lighter fabrics meant that even stays were not always needed for those with a slimmer or more slight figure. Nevertheless, because of the climate, women often resorted to an undergarment which was essentially a version of the pantaloon in flesh-coloured stockinette for warmth.

Polaire, the French music hall entertainer, in an elegant white dress, typical of the later Victorian era, emphasizing her hourglass silhouette.

The hourglass silhouette

Victorian society seems to have viewed the natural female form of the early Regency period as vulgar, indecent, and unseemly. Yet it was during the Victorian era that, perhaps paradoxically, the fashion for an extreme hourglass female shape really came into its own.

By 1820, as the general fashion for a slimmer waistline once more came to the fore, women again took to the corset to achieve the desirable body shape of the day. A nipped-in waist was combined with wider skirts to further enhance the waist, and wide skirts were in turn balanced with a wider shoulder line. Fashions quickly moved on from the comfortable, natural, empire line style of the early years of the 19th century to a much more controlled, curvaceous figure. The vogue for a tiny waist, combined with wide shoulders and even wider skirts, created the illusion of an hourglass-shaped figure, a silhouette that was to become much beloved by Victorian society.

It was not, as it would be in the 20th century, seen as a sexy feminine shape, but rather as an indication of women's fertility and position in society as the mothers of the nation. Corsetry was used to reduce the waist to sometimes severe lengths while elevating the bust; crinolines and bustles further created a fuller, more maternal figure.

Elastic brings a degree of freedom

Inventor Thomas Hancock introduced elastic fabrics to the market place in the 1820s and by 1840 the new elastic laces allowed women to both put on and remove their corsets without the assistance of a maid. While most corsets were still sewn by hand by tailors, some ready-to-wear pieces started to become available during the mid-19th century. The advent of heavily steel-boned corsets with a metal front busk and the use of the revolutionary new metal eyelets at the back generated a general mass passion for the "wasp-waisted" figure.

Going to extremes

Enormous bell-shaped crinolines, highlighting a tiny waist, topped with a flamboyant explosion of ribbons and frills around the shoulders, created a most unnatural and thoroughly impractical look for the lady of leisure, with women finding it increasingly difficult to sit down or get through doorways, often with hilarious results. The morals of Victorian society are perhaps reflected in this example of the most extreme concealment of the female form. Beneath elaborate constructions of steel overlaid with layer upon layer of fabric and extravagant ornamentation, the soft female body can barely be imagined in its natural state.

Shockingly, the Victorian attitude towards women's sexuality extended to a requirement to disguise the pregnant form with the use of corsetry.

Although the Victorians delighted in sentimental imagery of mothers and children, standards of decency meant that the reality of the expanding waistline of the pregnant female was considered so undesirable that corsets were designed specifically for wear during pregnancy. As it was considered an unwelcome reminder of women's carnal urges, pregnancy was not even discussed in polite company, and women were expected to remove themselves almost entirely from society. Although the ideal virtues required of the Victorian wife were that she was domestic, compliant, obedient, and fertile, the reality of producing children flew in the face of the prevailing fantasy of the innocence and respectability of the married woman and the self-control and civilized nature of the Victorian male.

Toward the end of the 19th century a certain hysteria grew around both the fad for tightlacing and corset wearing in general. Doctors reported cases of severe damage to the health, even the deaths of those using the corset. Women who practised tightlacing were vilified and condemned for their vanity and foolishness.

CORSET DE JEUNE FILLE. — Long, mince, fin g, toujours e. coutil blanc avec chaste broderie faisant la poi hier le devant. « Ne la serrez pas », dit invariablement n. m. n. vx ites-moi bien mince », implore la jeune fille. Leur rê e à toutes est d'avoir 48 de tour de taille. Mais, petite malheu euse, une taille bien ronde qui mesure 58, un contour de poitri e qui att int 110

.s jeunes filles, n'impressionneront .es dentelles d'une blancheur imma ne blague pas tant que ça, vous s qui vous donne ses vingt ans, acco dot !

1892 illustration showing the corset a women wears as a young girl, the one she wears as a bride, and the one she wears when she becomes pregnant, aimed to conceal her pregnant figure.

CORSET DE MARIEE. — Sera toujours de bon goût, véritablement élégant ; en moire blanche rabattue d'un volant d'Alençon, avec le jupon également en moire à *larges créneaux* découpés sur un haut volant d'alençon. Toutes les fantaisies *clair de lune*, *rose effeuillée*, qui séduisent un mari comme ces soies, blême... parfaitement. On rant une belle jeune fille souvent d'une fort belle

SIX MOIS APRÈS. — On lui demande toujours le secret de ses espérances. — Un garçon ? nous le ferons en satin bleu. — Une fille ? En satin rose. Et les hanches peuvent se développer sans gêne ni compression sous les larges et souples élastiques de soie rose ou bleue qui sont posés entre les baleines et qui suivront le développement du corps. Très élégamment garni de dentelle C'est déjà assez triste d'être déformée...

Tightlacing

The social reformer B. O. Flower condemned the practice of tightlacing:

The learned Doctor Trall in writing on this subject wisely observes: The evil effects of tightlacing, or of lacing at all, and of binding the clothing around the hips, instead of suspending it from the shoulders, can never be fully realized without a thorough education in anatomy and physiology. It is obvious that, if the diameter of the chest, at its lower and broader part, is diminished by lacing, or any other cause, to the extent of one fourth or one half, the lungs are pressed in towards the heart, the lower ribs are drawn together and press on the liver, and spleen, while the abdominal organs are pressed downwards on the pelvic viscera. The stomach is compressed in its transverse diameter; both the stomach, upper intestines, and liver are pressed downward on the kidneys, and on the lower portions of the bowels while the bowels are crowded down on the uterus and bladder, Thus every vital organ is either functionally obstructed or mechanically disordered, and diseases more or less aggravated, the condition of all. In post-mortem examinations the liver has been found deeply indented by the constant and prolonged pressure of the ribs, in consequence of tightlacing. The brain-organ, protected by a bony inclosure, has not yet been distorted externally by the contrivances of milliners and mantua-makers; but lacing the chest, by interrupting the circulation of the blood, prevents its free return from the vessel of the brain, and so permanent congestion of that organ, with constant liability to headache, vertigo, or worse affections, becomes a "second nature." The vital resources of every person, and all available powers of mind and body, are measurable by the respiration. Precisely as the breathing is lessened, the length of life is shortened; not only this, but life is rendered correspondingly useless and miserable while it does exist. It is impossible for any child, whose mother has diminished her breathing capacity by lacing, to have a sound and vigorous organization. If girls will persist in ruining their vital organs as they grow up to womanhood. No woman can ever forget the pain she endured when she first applied the corsets; but in time the compressed organs become torpid; the muscles lose their contractile power, and she feels dependent on the mechanical support of the corset. But the mischief is not limited to local weakness and insensibility. The general strength and general sensibility correspond with the breathing capacity. If she has diminished her "breath of life", she has just to that extent destroyed all normal sensibility. She can neither feel nor think normally. But in place of pleasurable sensations and ennobling thoughts, are an indescribable array of aches, pains, weaknesses, irritations, and nameless distresses of body, with dreamy vagaries, fitful impulses, and morbid sentimentalities of mind. And yet another evil is to be mentioned to render the catalogue complete. Every particle of food must be aerated in the lungs before it can be assimilated. It follows, therefore, that no one can be well nourished who has not a full, free, and unimpeded action of the lungs. In the contracted chest, the external measurement is reduced one half; but as the upper portions of the lungs cannot be fully inflated until the lower portions are fully expanded, it follows that the breathing capacity is diminished more than one half. It is wonderful how anyone can endure existence, or long survive, in this devitalized condition; yet, thousands do, and with careful nursing, manage to bring into the world several sickly children. The spinal distortion is one of the ordinary consequences of lacing. No one who laces habitually can have a straight or strong back.

B. O. Flower, Fashion Slaves*, 1891.*

EFFECT OF AN **OLD STYLE CORSET**

THE NEW FIG-URE

Illustration from the Ladies Home Journal, *October 1900, contrasting the old Victorian corseted silhouette with the new Edwardian "S-bend" corseted silhouette.*

The "S-bend" silhouette

Later in the 19th century, the vast crinolines of the 1850s and 1860s were replaced by the bustle, whereby most of the emphasis was put on the back of the skirt with elaborate ruching and padding to give the desired outline. This gave the wearer a softer, "S"-shaped silhouette, which described the woman's shape in side view.

Bustles of the time were many and varied, incorporating a number of novel features. The "New Phantom Bustle," for example, had pivoted steel wiring to support the bustle that was designed to fold in on itself when the wearer was seated and spring back into place on arising. And some bustles manufactured around the time of the Queen's Golden Jubilee even featured a musical box which played "God Save The Queen" whenever the wearer sat down.

The new "S-bend" look was celebrated by American illustrator Charles Dana Gibson in his "Gibson Girls" creations which featured in many publications of the day and became a model for femininity of the times. This new woman, who could still be considered a beauty while taking part in sports and generally being competitive, was truly revolutionary. The dawn of the girdle, brassières, cami knickers and a new willowy, even boyish figure was just around the corner.

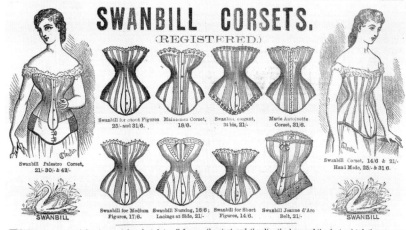

THAT the same make of Corset cannot be adapted to all figures—the stout and the slim, the long and the short waisted, the naturally graceful and the figures that obviously stand in need of being made so—seems so much of a truism that it would need an apology for stating it, were it not that it is claimed for the many so-called "inventions" which are now before the public.

It will surely occur to every lady who gives the matter a thought that the only sensible and simple plan, in order to be really " bien corseté," is to visit an establishment where are to be found the outcome of the study and practical skill of the leading Corsetières, where a lady can see and have explained to her the various excellencies and advantages of different types of Corsets, and where, above all, they will have the experienced advice of a Practical French Staymaker, who will advise them as to the Corset exactly adapted to their type of figure.

Descriptive Key of Forty different Corsets post free.

Sous la Direction d'une Corsetiere Parisienne.   Send Size of Waist with P.O. Order to prevent delay and inconvenience

Mrs ADDLEY BOURNE,
LADIES' OUTFITTER, CORSET AND BABY LINEN MANUFACTURER,
37, PICCADILLY (Opposite St James's Church), LONDON.

*Mrs Addley Bourne advertises
her "Swanbill" corsets at her shop
in Piccadilly, 1879.*

A new kind of corset

Even before World War One, fashionable clothing styles had begun to integrate a lower waistline. As a result, corsets became longer, even covering the thighs. The nipped-in waist was completely abandoned and the elegant shape of the time was slender, small-breasted, long-legged, and slim-hipped.

The straight-fronted or "swan bill" corset fashionable from 1900 to 1910 was a tight-laced corset with a long, firm, straight busk down the centre at the front which uncomfortably prodded into the groin area, encouraging the pelvis to retreat. This lifted the breasts upwards, the torso forwards and the hips backwards, thus giving an illusion of a smaller waist. It was suggested that this was a "healthy corset," as it produced less compression of the abdomen.

The decline of the corset

The invention of the "healthy corset" was only the start of a period of ingenuity and modernization which resulted in the arrival of the girdle, the brassière, cami knickers, stockings, and the development of mass production techniques for lingerie for the first time. But corsets did not disappear overnight. Various manufacturers were competing for the lucrative new market in healthier corsets, with fashionable long-line shapes, and shoulder straps giving more support for the bust and the back. Many of these new corset designs incorporated elastic side-lacing for comfort, with cording or stiff fabric strips replacing boning, and often including a garter belt. Eventually, the tight-laced, long-line, "swan bill" corset was abandoned for more free-flowing lingerie, in keeping with the liberated times.

Brave new world

Throughout the 20th century, the ideal female body image has swung from slim and svelte to shapely and curvaceous, depending on a variety of social and political forces. At the turn of the century, women's position in society was evolving; a significant number were entering higher education and joining the workplace. The notion that women were the weak and frail sex was losing momentum. Women began participating in sports, and a fashion for a more athletic, slender figure took the place of the Victorian ideal of a full bosom, tiny waist, and expansive hips. The highly structured corsets of the Victorian era, which were intended to produce an hourglass shape, were replaced with designs which encouraged an upright but slim figure.

The reign of the popular monarch King Edward VII saw the beginning of the end of the British Empire, which had reached its zenith during Queen Victoria's lifetime, and the dawn of what was a new optimism born out of a time of modernization and plenty, commonly referred to as "La Belle

Epoque." J. B. Priestley described the era as "the lost golden age ... all the more radiant because it is on the other side of the huge black pit of war."

This period was also the point at which the demand for universal female suffrage was gaining support in parliament and gathered unstoppable momentum. The calls for female emancipation and the immense changes on the horizon were inevitably reflected in the styles and fashions of the day. Later, the need for freer movement necessitated by women's work in the war had an even greater impact.

A need for practicality

Since the Middle Ages women's fashions have focused on the physical distinctions between the sexes. However, with World War One and the requirement for women to become part of the workforce, this was no longer the case. An army of women who were employed in armaments factories, driving delivery trucks and harvesting crops now needed the freedom of movement which more practical clothing provided.

This resulted in women wearing shorter skirts, even trousers and breeches, all in lighter, more easily cleaned fabrics. Corsets became smaller and more pliable. Girdles and short corsets were the viable alternative to the traditional corset and as a result the all-important brassière also became an essential item in the lingerie wardrobe.

Judy Oswald modeling a Poiret evening outfit, 1913. Paul Poiret was "the man who at the turn of the century got women out of the bones and hourglass padding of the past. He invented the 20th century look." London Daily News.

Poiret's radical designs

French designer Paul Poiret was responsible for a dramatic change in tailoring, with his introduction of simple designs like harem pants and lampshade tunics which featured his radical draping techniques. Poiret is credited with liberating women from their corsets with his loose, unfettered silhouette and is acknowledged as the designer of the first shapewear. His designs were less about waist cinching and more about the fabric hugging the figure, and creating a sensual curve around the hips and buttocks.

Although there is little evidence to support the theory, many clothing historians believe that Poiret developed a rubber girdle to wear as a support garment underneath his stunning creations. His flowing dresses and draped fabrics inspired by Art Deco shapes and designs heralded a new modernity, not only changing women's views on clothing, but allowing a new more liberated way of moving and, by extension, living.

Flappers and the boyish outline

With the 1920s, the straight-up-and-down, flat-chested, "flapper girl" arrived, with her short shift dresses, bobbed hair styles, and very little requirement for corsets or shape-changing foundation garments, given the trend for loose-fitting dresses. The "flapper" fashions of the 1920s were partly a rebellion on the part of women who had experienced their first

La toile de soie rayée

La toile de soie rayée, dresses in summer fashions in striped silk, May 1925. Woment wearing typical 1920s straight shift dresses and cloche hats.

their first taste of emancipation during wartime, when they had played a vital role in keeping factories and industry functioning. These newly empowered women were not all happy to return to the domestic role of wife and mother, and their defiance was apparent in their unconventional look. They smoked cigarettes, wore trousers, cut their hair in short, sleek boyish styles, wore revealing, sleeveless shift dresses, exposing tanned and toned arms, and topped off the new look with a bust-reducing bra to give the appearance of a flat chest.

The 1920s were also the beginning of fashion for all. Readily available patterns for simple straight shift dresses meant that these sophisticated styles could be easily made at home and were available to all classes: High fashion was no longer the preserve of the aristocracy.

Corsets all but disappear

Although the bras of the time were often used to flatten the chest to give a more boyish look, corsets which not only held in the tummy but held up the stockings were demoted from waist cincher to suspender belt.

Given the fashionable shape of the time, corset sales dropped by around 70 per cent during the 1920s, and, if they were worn at all, the new, more comfortable "lastex" girdles were preferred to the traditional long-line corset for the purpose of flattening the abdomen. The first roll-on girdle

Hollywood actress Ava Gardner in a dress cinched in at the waist, typical of the early Hollywood fashions designed to highlight the feminine figure.

in 1932 was most popular with younger women and those with a slighter figure who required only light control. These roll-on girdles remained popular for many years and went on to become the most celebrated light-control wear of the era.

The return of femininity

The 1930s saw a more feminine hourglass shape in fashion once again. Women were inspired to celebrate their curves and, given the fabulous new wardrobe of lingerie available to them, they wholeheartedly embraced the opportunity. New manufacturing techniques and elastic stretch fabrics allowed the mass production of figure-hugging girdles, paneled brassières and attractive and functional garter belts.

The glamor reflected on the silver screen was the perfect escape from the poverty and deprivation of the Great Depression. The Hollywood studios understood that the styles worn by their top stars would be emulated by women around the globe, and they possessed the world's most powerful marketing tool: the movies. Between the wars, Hollywood cemented its position as the epitome of style and of all things glossy and dazzling.

World War Two put a halt to all but essential manufacture for the war effort. Corset and bra manufacturing were effectively banned as the component parts of rubber and steel were at a premium. "Make do

Benice Swanson wearing sweater girl jeansand a close fitted top, typical of the 1950s "preppy" look.

and mend" including "stockings" created by applying leg make-up and homemade undergarments re-fashioned from old clothes or parachute silk, epitomized the mood of the times.

Teenage trends

Following World War Two, the emergence of the idea of the teenager as a separate life stage between childhood and adulthood created a whole new marketing opportunity for the burgeoning German and American lingerie industries.

Sexy screen sirens like Jane Russell and Marilyn Monroe in Hollywood movies set the fashion for skin-tight sweaters and so-called bullet bras, while singers Connie Francis and Brenda Lee spoke to a generation of teenage girls who rejected the styles of their mothers. With disposable income and a rebellious outlook, they demanded fashion which was fun, affordable and, above all, their own. A specifically teenage "preppy"look, popularized by music, movies and television stars, included circle skirts and close-fitting tops and trousers. By this time, teenage girls could buy an impressive range of well-fitting bras, garter belts and even girdles from a wide range of manufacturers at any Main Street store. The traditional corset already seemed like a thing of the past.

Mary Quant, UK fashion designer wearing her own designs and with bob haircut at her Knightsbridge boutique Bazaar, London 1966.

Mary Quant

It's now more than 40 years since the Goldsmiths' art student put together her first collection of mini dresses and skirts, with the backing of her husband and business partner, Alexander Plunkett Greene. At the time, the style created a hullabaloo. In the decades since, hems have dropped, risen and sometimes disappeared entirely. Is she surprised that what now looks like a relatively modest garment still receives so much attention and acclaim? "Well, I know everybody loves it, everybody loves wearing it, it makes people feel happy somehow, and I'm delighted with that", she says. And it was a big breakthrough. It was perfect because it was the feeling of the time and everything was so right for it.

Kate Finnigan interview with Mary Quant in the Daily Telegraph, *11 January 2009.*

Rebellion against tradition

By the mid-1960s the feminist movement was in full flow and many women felt an important sign of their liberation was, figuratively at least, to burn their bra, ditch their girdle and bin their stockings, and to promote a more liberated and less overtly sexual image of womanhood. The symbolic act of throwing away the garments which were regarded by many as hallmarks of women's subservience was in reality a scalding critique of the patriachal society of the times, and the prevailing beauty culture which valued women only for their looks, and not for their brains and abilities. It was also clearly a rebellion against the age-old traditions of cinching, padding, pushing, restraining and compressing, in order to produce a female silhouette of which society might approve.

New trends, new technology

In spite of these revolutionary times, controlling foundation garments and even corsets were still sometimes worn; long-line bras that went all the way down to the waist remained popular, and padded latex foam bras were bestsellers. Nylon tights replaced stockings; freeing the thighs from suspender belts made it possible for the risqué and ever shorter mini skirt to take prime position in the sixties' girl's wardrobe. Worn with knee high "kinky boots," bikini panties and nylons, the mini skirt, initially introduced by Mary Quant for the ultra-trendy Chelsea set in London, took the world by storm.

In 1964, the Canadelle company in Canada produced the first "Wonderbra," which was designed specifically to "lift and separate" the bust to give a firm, high, and sexy shape. This was followed by the Playtex "Cross Your Heart" bra in 1965, and their "18-hour girdle" in 1967. A host of contour and support undergarments for the modern woman followed.

At the same time, new developments in elastics technology, such as Lycra and Spanzelle, resulted in better-fitting and longer-lasting bras and girdles. These more durable and easier-to-care-for fabrics prompted a massive boom in sales of lingerie, and manufacturers, including Berlei, Lovable, Playtex and Marks & Spencer, reaped the benefits. By the 1970s Triumph had produced their first "soft cup" bra, the "Doreen" which provided substantial support without underwiring.

The decline of the girdle

A somewhat more natural female shape was considered chic; with the hippy look and the longer midi and maxi skirts in fashion, girdles and corsets became virtually obsolete. Sales of girdles took a nosedive, with women considering them to be both uncomfortably constraining and an unhealthy consequence of a fashion industry dominated by men. In spite of Playtex's ubiquitous marketing campaigns, and their product developments and refinements, girdles were seen as old-fashioned.

Although the more conventional fashions of the time still promoted slender hips and waist, with a large bosom, a good bra and a well-toned body were now more important in creating a fashionable shape.

A new vogue for keeping fit was embodied by one of the bestselling videos of 1982, *Jane Fonda's Workout*. The F-plan diet, fitness gurus, pumping iron, yoga and working out became buzz words for the woman of the 1980s, who expected to be able to diet and sculpt her body in order to look gorgeous in her clothing rather than relying on her underwear.

*Madonna in Jean Paul
Gaultier corset, on stage
during her Blond Ambition
world tour, 1990. Tour
designed by Jean Paul
Gaultier.*

Lingerie as outerwear

In the late 1980s, designers such as Jean Paul Gaultier and Vivienne Westwood heralded a renaissance of the corset. They both regarded the corset as a unique sculptural garment and introduced the post-modern idea of "underwear as outerwear" at a time when fashion had once more fallen in love with a more voluptuous female form. Their designs created a revolutionary new idea of the corset in which the powerful female body is simultaneously worshiped and restrained.

Fashion designers have increasingly thrived through creating and maintaining relationships with influential clients, whose prestige and high public profile give the popular seal of approval to designs which might otherwise be considered risqué. During her celebrated 1990 Blond Ambition tour, Madonna performed in a variety of flamboyant, sexy Gaultier creations including an outrageous gold corset with exaggerated conical breasts, and spectacular pieces worn as theatrical costume. Gaultier's example threw open the doors for other designers to follow.

When Mr. Pearl created the beaded corset for Victoria "Posh Spice" Beckham on her marriage, a whole generation of Spice Girl fans must have immediately started saving their allowances to get their hands on something that reflected its glamor. In recent times, even Stella McCartney, revered for her drapery and soft tailoring, has incorporated the corset into her more conservative collections, aimed more toward the businesswoman, and worn as part of a suit.

From fetish to mainstream

This universal acceptance of corset wearing as symbolic of power, potency, and exaggerated femininity has coincided with a renewed interest in tightlacing, extreme corset training, and fetish and erotic fashions. Rubber corsets, leather corsets, thigh-high boots, stilettos, bondage pants, wrist cuffs, and harnesses have all been integrated into the palette of the fashion designer. While previously, highly specialized rubber designers such as Atsuko Kudo would have appealed only to a select fetish market, now their designs are regularly featured across the pages of magazines including *Vogue, Harper's Bazaar* and the *Sunday Times.*

Over the past 100 years, corsets have moved in and out of fashion; at one time they almost disappeared altogether from our wardrobes. We now live in a period of tremendous choice and variety in our lingerie options, with girdles, corsets, bustiers, contour garments, and a wealth of technologically advanced shapewear available in every shopping mall. Whether the revival of corsetry since the 1980s is strictly a temporary fashion which will fade and change as all fashion does, or if it is indeed the incorporation of an irreplaceable piece of sculpting lingerie into our everyday attire, remains to be seen.

During the first decade of the 21st century it is indisputable that we have experienced an almost obsessive pursuit of a slender female body shape that has led many women toward extreme dieting, punishing exercise regimes, and even gastric surgery. For those who can, an expensive trip to a plastic surgeon, surgical implants, and liposuction have replaced working out at the gym. For those who cannot, there are power panties, body shapers, and push-up bras to achieve the desired effect. As I am often quoted as saying, "four months hard labor at the gym, or four inches of instant reduction with a corset" – for me, there really is no contest.

Model Bex Paul in vintage cotton print and duchess satin hourglass suspender corset, Velda Lauder "Mannikin" collection, 2008.

Model Mam'zelle Maz
dressed in classic demi cup,
long-line corset in silk and
eyelash lace, Velda lauder
"Salon de Tea" collection
2009.

Advertisement from November 1955, a chain store buyer says "women do not know their correct bust size," so they have devised a method for mesuring busts for curve-conscious women.

Modern Corset Culture

For much of the 20th century, it seemed that the corset had had its day. Changing fashions which required less rigid underpinning and advances in technology meant that, except for a brief period when Dior's New Look was in vogue, corsets were replaced by more flexible underwear and seemed to have been consigned to the closet of history. But the punk movement of the 1970s and its chief designer, Vivienne Westwood, reinterpreted the corset as outerwear and devotees of the new burlesque movement such as Dita Von Teese and Immodesty Blaize reinvented and revitalized the corset for a new generation.

The arrival of the brassière

ALTHOUGH WOMEN HAD USED binding, bands, bodices, and corsets through the ages to help reduce, increase or change the shape of the bustline, it was not until 1889 that the brassière came into being. Its creator was the Argentinian-born, Paris-based corsetière Herminie Cadolle who created a garment that we would recognize as the forerunner to the modern brassière. Known as the "Bien-être" or "Well-being," it was essentially a corset cut into two pieces; the upper part of the garment supported and lifted the bust using straps over the shoulders.

Further innovation and mass production

In 1893 Marie Tucek patented her "Breast Supporter" a foundation garment that had pouches specially designed for the breasts to sit in, and in 1907 *Vogue* first used the term "brassière" to describe the new innovation. In 1914 an American socialite called Mary Phelps Jacobs invented her own version. Her "Backless brassière," which she originally made out of two handkerchiefs tied together with ribbon for the straps, was registered with the U.S. patent office under her company name, Caresse Crosby. Phelps Jacobs went on to sell the brassière patent to the Warner Brothers Corset Company in Connecticut. They further developed the garment into the form we know today and made a small fortune from the design over the next 30 years.

The U.S.A. was the setting for another key development when, in New York in 1922, Ida Cohen Rosenthal produced a fitted brassière, with two cups, shoulder straps, and a band that fastened at the back. By 1928 she had also introduced the idea of cup sizes. Rosenthal then went on to establish the enormously successful Maidenform Brassière Company which manufactured and sold her products by the millions during the 1920s and 1930s.

New fabrics and cup sizes

The widespread use of new synthetic fabrics, such as rayon in lingerie manufacture, meant that at last attractive and flattering undergarments were not limited only to the wealthy. As rayon resembled satin and silk, the average woman could now afford soft, sexy lingerie of the type previously only available at great expense from exclusive shops.

The bra became a huge growth industry and throughout the 1930s new technologies and a growing band of manufacturers such as Triumph and Gossard produced innovations in the fabrics and colors available and developed new design techniques that resulted in padded bras, adjustable straps, and standardized cup sizes (at first A, B, C, D) which allowed women of all shapes and sizes to finally have a comfortably fitting brassière. The bra, the girdle, and the garter belt had effectively taken the place of the corset in the 20th-century woman's wardrobe.

Model Mam'zelle Maz poses in a soft mesh hanky bra, high-waisted girdle and shrug. Velda Lauder "Gothikka" collection, 2010.

Betty Grabble starring in "Tin Pan Alley," 1940.

The Hollywood effect

With every decade that passed Hollywood was able to successfully encapsulate and reflect back the dreams of the man and woman on the street. On-screen glamor and glitz provided the perfect escape from the Great Depression of the early 1930s, light relief during wartime, and a signal of the good times to come in the post-war years. In spite of a lack of disposable income, crowds flocked to the movies to escape their cares.

The Hollywood studios were well aware that the clothes, hair and make-up worn by their leading ladies quickly became the rage and could be used as a marketing tool in a movie's publicity campaign. Greta Garbo and Marlene Dietrich with their fine, arched eyebrows and shortwaved hairstyles; Veronica Lake's cascade of hair falling over one eye and the upswept coils of Betty Grable and Rita Hayworth were all fashionable styles that were emulated by women around the world.

Women in movies were celebrated, esteemed, and powerful: from the formidable, business-like Katharine Hepburn to the thrillingly enigmatic Greta Garbo, the fascination they held for the general public was matched only by royalty and the aristocracy. The love affair between Edward VIII and Wallis Simpson provided a spectacular media circus in the 1930s, and the couple went on to figure among the most influential style icons of the era.

The arrival of austerity

With the outbreak of World War Two, a period of austerity and shortages halted any further developments in lingerie and a more utilitarian approach was adopted across the board. Women once again took on the jobs of the men who had gone to war, and even the future monarch, Princess Elizabeth, drove an army truck. As a result, functional designs, homemade garments, the re-use of fabric from such unexpected sources as salvaged silk parachutes and an attitude of make do and mend were the themes of the war effort.

During wartime, shortages in materials such as rubber, silk, and cotton encouraged clothing manufacturers to make advances in the development of alternative, synthetic fabrics. This innovation through necessity led to the introduction of Dunlop's Lastex into lingerie design. The liquid latex-

Jane Russell in her iconic pose from "The Outlaw," 1941.

based yarn was used in the manufacture of brassières and the elastic panels of girdles and allowed for a more comfortable and figure hugging fit.

Sweater girl chic and the cone bra

The impact of undergarments that fitted so closely to the contours of a women's body was reflected in the fashions worn by Hollywood glamor goddesses. They included Lana Turner who made famous the "sweater girl" chic of the 1940s and early 1950s and the torpedo-breasted pin-up girl style of Jane Russell and Marilyn Monroe which insured the phenomenal success of the bullet or "cone bra" as Hollywood continued to exert an enormously powerful influence over women's fashion. Jane Russell, with her 38-inch bust, famously co-starred in the 1941 film *The Outlaw* which was banned from general release for a full five years because the censors considered it to be thoroughly indecent, due in no small part to the movie's emphasis on the star's ample bosom.

Bras with large, pointy cups and girdles were seen in movies across the globe. The most popular bras of the time used the technique of circular top stitching to create cups which fitted well and gave a pleasing shape to the bust. The "bullet bra" was a conically-shaped bra that produced the definitive voluptuous, "breasts like missile silos" silhouette of the post-war years, topping off the new slinky sexy look.

The New Look: the feminine revived

"A golden age seemed to have come again. War had passed out of sight and there were no other wars on the horizon. What did the weight of my sumptuous materials, my heavy velvets and brocades, matter? When the hearts were light, mere fabrics could not weigh the body down. In December 1946, as a result of the war and uniforms, women still looked and dressed like Amazons. I designed clothes for flower-like women, with rounded shoulders, full feminine busts, and hand-span waists above enormous spreading skirts …"

Christian Dior quoted in The Golden Age of Couture: Paris and London 1947–1957.

New Look underwear circa 1947. Guipiere designed by Marie Rose Lebigot for Marcel Rochas.

A new age of style

The period from 1947 to 1957 is often referred to as the renaissance of or the "golden age of couture." In his 1947 collection Christian Dior banished the short skirts of wartime austerity when he introduced his "New Look." He showcased a selection of fabulous and luxurious full-length gowns with wide skirts, padded hips, and cinched waists, accessorized by chic little hats and full-length gloves.

The sheer flamboyance of the collection was considered by some as scandalous given the extravagant quantities of fabric used, which would have been quite impossible during the war years. However, Dior's new creations were designed to make his wealthy clients look and feel like seductive and glamorous sirens. The voluptuous, feminine look required controlling foundation garments, which Dior incorporated into his designs with the use of reinforced strong fabric, underwiring, bodices, bustiers, and traditional corsetry; either as an integral part of the costume or as a separate garment to be worn with the outfit.

New undies for a new silhouette

With conventional foundation garments making a comeback, the Warner Brothers' Corset Company obliged by creating the long-line, strapless, and boned "Merry Widow" corselette in 1952. This one-piece bra and girdle combination was boned with nine long spiral wires wrapped in satin, with black and white lace and elastane panels, and a large zip at the back that made a superbly controlling garment.

Launched to coincide with the release of the Lana Turner movie of the same name and extensively worn by Turner in the film, the "Merry Widow" was the perfect synthesis of branding and marketing between Hollywood and lingerie manufacturers. The corset featured in much of the movie's advertising and was pitched as a sexy, racy, and glamorous undergarment, although it was apparently particularly uncomfortable to wear. Lana Turner is quoted as saying, "I'm telling you – the "Merry Widow" was designed by a man. A woman would never do that to another woman."

Although the New Look's elaborate creations may have dominated the couture scene at the time, there are several other styles and silhouettes that remain firmly associated with the 1950s. Ava Gardner, Rita Hayworth, Grace Kelly, and numerous New York socialites were dressed by Dior, but Audrey Hepburn and Leslie Caron opted for a simpler, more chic style. At the other end of the spectrum stars such as Doris Day and Debbie Reynolds represented a more conservative, everyday look aimed at the average woman.

During the mid-1950s, in stark contrast to Dior's elaborate designs which had dominated the couture scene, Coco Chanel introduced her new suit design. Of textured tweed, braid trimmed, with a collarless jacket and knee length skirt, this classic, smart, yet formal look was immensely popular for its understated elegance and timeless style. The Chanel look remained popular right through the 1960s when glamor and sophistication was rapidly replaced with new innovation, radical ideas, and space age styles.

The rise of the teenager

The popularity of Elvis Presley and the rock and roll era heralded a period of adolescent rebellion; girls no longer wanted to look like their mothers and sought out a more youthful look. Fashion was fun and affordable to the youth of the 1950s and many young girls emulated teen idols such as Connie Francis and Brenda Lee. The rise of the "teenager" as a new market for sales created an explosion of polyester and nylon "preppy" clothing: circle skirts, bobby socks, close fitting tops, and narrow trousers for girls were amongst the most popular looks. The values of humility and self-effacement previously considered most attractive in the female, were replaced with a new model of assertive self-determination and, most importantly, spending power.

The comfortable girdle

"My girdle is killing me."
(Voice-over) : "She needs
the new 18-hour girdle by
Playtex. It's made from a
remarkable new fabric Playtex
just invented. A delicate
weaving with the strength to
hold you firm all day. The
first firm control girdle that's
comfortable for hours. The
new 18-hour girdle — by
Playtex."

Playtex Girdle advert, 1967.

Maudie Edwards dressing in a girdle, from the 1952 film "Girle of Gold."

Sixties shapewear

The 1960s introduced many households to the pleasures of consumerism as many found themselves benefiting from increased disposable income. Both young and old were able to indulge in an era of plenty with an abandonment that previous generations could only have dreamed of. A new wardrobe of softer, lighter, stylish and sensual lingerie was within the grasp of practically every woman and teenager. New lightweight, but fully supportive, bras with adjustable elastic straps and plastic rather than metal wiring, were gratefully embraced by these avid consumers.

New bras and the 18-hour girdle

In 1962 Dimanche created the first seamless bra, which was perfect for wearing under figure-hugging tops and dresses. By 1964 the Canadelle company had produced the first "Wonderbra" with its emphasis on lifting and separating the bust. In 1965 Playtex countered with their "Cross Your Heart" bra and in 1967 they produced another worldwide hit with their "18-hour girdle". Using new and revolutionary fabrics such as latex, lycra, and nylon resulted in better fitting and longer lasting underwear that was lightweight and easy to clean. The lingerie market exploded with new innovative designs and constructions and manufacturers were able to indulge in extravagant, experimental, and raunchy marketing campaigns to encourage the 1960s woman to buy their new creations.

Playtex were the world leaders in girdle design, manufacture, and distribution with their seamless and figure-controlling shapewear. When they introduced their latex and fabricon, micro perforated "18 hour girdle" with a firm control panel over the tummy, it was marketed as being so incredibly comfortable and light that you could wear it all day and night. There was a design to suit every occasion, from the shorter waist to thigh versions, to the full-length all in one.

Despite the manufacturer's extravagant claims these garments were manufactured from latex, and despite the numerous tiny perforations in the fabric, they could be sweaty and uncomfortable with a tendency to split as the latex degraded with age. Playtex did not dwell on the drawbacks and their famous marketing know-how gave rise to some very memorable advertising campaigns including the infamous, "My girdle is killing me" advertisement (see page 96).

The "Cross Your Heart" bra and the "I Can't Believe it's a Girdle" design in a more durable weave and lycra, further cemented Playtex's position as market leaders. This lightweight, well-constructed, machine-washable shapewear perfectly met 1960s women's requirements for simple, labor-saving devices which made her life easier and less complicated.

The pill and the sexual revolution

The contraceptive pill was introduced to Britain in 1961 and it has often been suggested that the extra quantities of the hormone estrogen that were introduced into the body, had the unexpected side-effect of increasing the bust measurements of young girls by around an inch over the next 20 years. Between 1962 and 1969 the take-up figures of the first pill increased from around 50,000 to one million in the U.K and the sexual revolution that followed paved the way for the more extreme and overtly sexual popular fashions which followed.

The mood of "Swinging Sixties" fashion was epitomized by designers such as the U.K.'s Mary Quant and France's André Courrèges whose mini skirts and Mod look caused a sensation. Prior to the 1960s short skirts had been used only as sports attire; when Quant launched her racy new mini designs she unsurprisingly caused enormous controversy.

These super-short skirts, some less than 16 inches long, were made possible only by the introduction of nylon panty hose. Without the need for garters to hold the stockings up, the thigh could be on full display right up to the panty line. Furthermore, panty hose retailed for about a quarter of the price of a pair of stockings and were an overnight success. In London, bowler-hatted businessmen banged their umbrellas on the boutique's windows in disgust at the indecent mini skirt.

Colin Rolfe's mini shift dress, which was modelled by Jean Shrimpton at Derby Day in Melbourne, Australia in 1965, left onlookers aghast at the

Sid Vicious of punk band the Sex Pistols with girlfriend Nancy Spungen, in typical punk dress, 1970.

sheer brevity of its design, but hipsters and ardent feminists seem to have considered the look to be liberating and happening.

Writing in *Oz* magazine in February 1969, Germaine Greer commented: "women kept on dancing. Their long skirts crept up, their girdles dissolved, their nipples burst through like hyacinth tips and their clothes withered away to the mere wisps and ghosts of draperies to adorn and glorify ..."

Vivienne Westwood and punk fashion

Vivienne Westwood is regarded as the mother of the punk movement in fashion. In the 1970s she created and invented an entirely new and challenging look which was to change the way we look at fashion forever. While her then boyfriend, Malcolm McLaren pioneered his vision of a new punk sound with the Sex Pistols, the band he assembled from the members of a band called the Strand who regularly hung around at Westwood's "SEX" boutique on the King's Road, Westwood worked on her new anti-fashion designs and an enduring new cultural era was born. Punk was Westwood's backlash to the Sixties and she is quoted as saying that she wanted to "tighten it all up, pull it in... be direct and stern."

SEX sold her unique take on classic fetish rubber clothing, bondage gear, and the then notorious Tom of Finland T-shirts featuring two naked cowboys. An antiestablishment ethos as the essential core of her initial collections, liberated the secret world of fetish garb, and the clothing of the fetishist and sadomasochist underworld surfaced into mainstream society. In her subsequent collections rubber and studs gave way to her take on 18th-century corsetry, and jeweled codpieces and towering shoes continued her fetishistic themes. For Westwood corsetry was deliberately created as outer wear and firmly put on the fashion map. Along with bondage gear the corset was freed from the fetish closet and found its place in the fashion arena.

The revival of the corset

Ted Polhemus, an American photographer, anthropologist and writer based in the U.K., has described Goth fashion as "a profusion of black velvets, lace, fishnets and leather tinged with scarlet or purple, accessorised with tightly-laced corsets, gloves, precarious stilettos and silver jewelry depicting religious or occult themes."

Goth fashion began in the U.K. in the early 1980s and was initially associated with gothic rock music. Classic Goth looks feature back-combed and crimped hair dyed red, purple or black; very pale, often white, foundation and heavy black eyeliner with purple and deepest red lipstick. The style includes Victorian and Edwardian-style clothing mixed

Goth Girl poses in Camden Market, London, in the 1980s.

Model Mam'zelle Maz wears soft mesh hanky bra, jet swarovski crystal mesh corset and power mesh skirt, Velda Lauder "Gothikka" collection, 2010.

with punk and fetish influences, often displaying dark, morbid and erotic themes–perfect for the inclusion of the corset.

I witnesssed the last days of the early London Goth scene, and came across my first examples of reconstructed corsets. Facsimiles of Victorian and Edwardian corsets danced around darkened nightclub rooms to gothic dirges, and my fascination began. Goth fashions subsequently transformed and metamorphosized, soon surreal color and cartoon elements came to punctuate the monochrome palette of the early years, but the corset has remained a constant throughout. Goth fashion is still a worldwide cultural phenomenon and one of the longest-lasting subcultures of the 20th century. It continues to diversify and evolve, constantly throwing up new subdivisions such as Cyber Goth, Emo, Death Rock and Goth Punk. Corsets continue to feature heavily in the latest incarnations of the Goth scene in the growing "Steam Punk" movement.

21st-century pin-up culture

Born Heather Sweet in Michigan, U.S.A, on September 28, 1972, a typical blonde mid-Western girl Dita Von Teese has reinvented and remodelled herself into a "Burlesque Superheroine" *(Vanity Fair, 2006)*. Perhaps surprisingly, Dita's audience and followers are mostly women,

*Grey and black satin
"curve" corset designed
for Dita Von Teese, Velda
Lauder, 2005.*

who see in her a new form of inspirational femininity. Identifiably both chic and sensual, she represents an alternative to the typical tall, tanned, blonde, pneumatic American ideal. Dita's flawless styling and exquisite performances, while initially classed as "niche" have gained her the accolades of admirers all over the world and given women permission to enjoy a retro guise complete with corset.

Dita Von Teese was an early fetish model for journals like *Skin 2* and *Marquis* magazine. Many of Dita's early fetish shoots were rubber themed, with Dita apparently drawing inspiration from the queen of the 1950s pin-ups, Bettie Page. Known for her naughty bondage-based photo-shoots combined with a sweet smile, Bettie is also a corset-wearing icon and inspiration for the current burlesque generation.

Dita Von Teese and the revival of burlesque

Dita seems to have had a life-long fascination with lingerie and vintage fashion, and has raised the profile of corsets with her extensive modeling and the use of corsets in her perfomance costumes. Her obvious interest in the Golden Age of Hollywood undoubtedly led to a fascination with 1940s movies and classic retro styles. She has developed her own unique style which has contributed significantly to the neo-burlesque explosion. Her alabaster skin, raven smooth locks, signature red lips, and beauty spot, are striking and seductive.

Iconic American pin-up glamor model Bettie Page in a "Tarzan" like pose on a modelling assignment in Africa, 1950.

Dita Von Teese shows are legendary, incorporating sumptuous corsets and costumes, alongside huge props such as her famous Martini glass, crystalized carousel horse, and an elaborate ornate Opium Den. A star of screen and catwalk, Dita has modeled for Vivienne Westwood, Jean Paul Gaultier, and designed for Wonderbra. She has published books on fetish, burlesque, and striptease, and was a Viva Glam spokesperson for MAC cosmetics. Acknowledged as the undisputed Queen of Burlesque, she has made a monumental journey from rubber fetish model to burlesque diva. Currently the most in-demand burlesque performer across the globe, her influence is worldwide, nowhere more so than in the U.K.

The advent of this modern-day glamor goddess has unequivocally heralded the return of the corset as a must-have item in most women's wardrobes. The New Burlesque scene puts style before striptease and vaudeville before overt erotica. Encompassing a wide range of performance styles from fun and humor, to melodrama, this scene has provided a platform for women to express their inner goddess in a light-hearted and supportive environment, allowing them to reclaim the corset on their own terms as a garment for expressing their mood and another item in their costume box.

The New Burlesque is a revival of the classic American burlesque striptease of the early half of the 20th century, first brought to America from Britain in the late 1860s by Lydia Thompson. The classical burlesque form is, however, both a British and European theatrical tradition, with the American burlesque tradition evolving through vaudeville.

Back detail from Velda Lauder "Gothikka" collection 2010. Modeled by Bex Paul and Mam'zelle Maz.

Mam'zelle Maz poses in underbust silk and eyelash applique lace corset and accessories, Velda Lauder "Salon de Tea" collection, 2009.

Deanne Lula Lee poses in red satin, black lace "curve" corset, Velda Lauder "Burlesque" collection, 2006.

Vaudeville and burlesque

Vaudeville was a form of variety performance that first appeared in New York in the early 1880s and was popular until the 1930s. The name vaudeville is believed to come from the term "voix de ville," which translates as "voice of the city" or alternatively "vaux de ville" meaning "worthy of the city." Vaudeville grouped together a number of unrelated variety acts which were often as diverse as comedians, acrobats, performing animals, magicians, short plays, and burlesque acts. Touring vaudeville companies successfully performed in huge theaters across North America until the early 1930s when the genre was gradually usurped by the popularity of movies, radio and the effect of widespread poverty during the Great Depression years. Vaudeville is still credited with having a strong influence on American comedy across a range of media.

During its heyday vaudeville provided a platform for burlesque artists to perform, among them is the legendary Gypsy Rose Lee, a major inspiration for most of today's showgirls and burlesque stars. Her slow, classy style of striptease allowed her to raise her performance to an altogether different level from most strip artists and to carve out a niche that was all her own. Born Rose Louise Hovick in 1911, Gypsy Rose Lee was a headliner at Minsky's and the Ziegfeld Follies, wrote three novels and starred in many movies and television programs. Although she died of lung cancer in 1970, her memory is very much alive today within the burlesque community and she is a constant inspiration for a new generation of performers.

Burlesque artist Immodesty Blaize performs on stage at KOKO, London, in 2009.

Immodesty Blaize and the new burlesque

The new burlesque features big bands, chorus girls, cabaret and humor. It is frequently a spectacular collection of visual delights distilled from the glamorous essence of the Parisian and Las Vegas showgirls. Immodesty Blaize is known as "the undisputed Queen of British burlesque" and cites movies such as *Gypsy* (based on the memoirs of Gypsy Rose Lee) as the inspiration for her illustrious career in burlesque. Today she is credited as one of the major instigators of the burlesque renaissance. Famous for her huge glittering telephone props and giant rocking horse act, Ms. Blaize is stunningly statuesque with an incredibly curvaceous body. In 2007 she was crowned Miss Exotic World.

The Miss Exotic World Pageant is of great significance to the burlesque community, and winning the pageant is considered the top honor for a burlesque performer. The pageant is a major inspiration for all showgirls; its creation has considerably contributed to the rise of the New Burlesque culture which has heralded a craze for corsets and retro lingerie. The spectacle of the showgirl's stage costumes has inspired a new era in fashion for corset as outer wear and retro lingerie as underwear.

In the U.K, there has been a burgeoning of interest in burlesque, with burlesque schools, fan dance classes and even "burlesquercise" classes cropping up nationwide. Vintage fashion and hairstyling, fascinator and nipple tassel workshops, are all part of the new cottage industries orbiting in the galaxy of sparkle that is the burlesque universe.

Cover illustration by John Willie for Bizarre, reproduced in first edition of ASG, 1974.
© *Bizarre Publishing Company.*

The Corset as Fetish Object

The concept of tightlacing as a fetish is first documented in the mid-19th century, but the idea of the corset as part of an explicit fetish scene is very much a later 20th century one. The artist John Willie's 1950s cartoon creation, Sweet Gwendoline was frequently drawn attired in the tightest of corsets, while a number of modern tightlacing practitioners such as Ethel Granger and Cathie Jung have pulled in their waists to the smallest proportions. Advances in rubber technology encouraged rubber enthusiasts to use the material to create a new generation of corsets, showcased at events such as the Torture Garden.

Vivienne Westwood leans against a telephone box with Jordan and another punk girl on a London street, 1977.

DESIGNER VIVIENNE WESTWOOD and the 1970s punk rock scene introduced fetish garments into the world of fashion and paved the way for overtly sexual clothing and fetish garments to be gradually integrated into mainstream fashion. Exemplified by high heels and corsets, quintessentially fetish items are now completely acceptable elements of many people's everyday wardrobe. From garbage bag-wearing punks loitering on the King's Road to the contemporary haute couture catwalk, fetish clothing is today very much part of mainstream fashion.

Suffering for beauty

As women will probably always be willing to endure a little discomfort to appear taller, thinner, more well-endowed, and younger, heels are getting higher and corsets tighter. Many humans' masochistic side is such that the pursuit of beauty will often involve enduring some discomfort in order to become something other than the ordinary self, emerging as a butterfly reborn into a new ideal of beauty. The process of transformation may sometimes require binding, Botox and branding, be it with tattoos or designer labels. Perhaps we are all slaves to vanity and the promise of constant reinvention.

The first documented reference to corsets in terms of fetishism appears in the mid-19th century in *The Englishwoman's Domestic Magazine*. Over 150 letters were received which detailed the practice of enforced extreme tightlacing in several boarding schools, often described as a useful method of controlling badly-behaved boys. Although later the letters' contents were dismissed as fantasy, they reveal the emergence of a sexual subculture in the grip of a tightlacing obsession.

This obsession has continued in contemporary society, finding a place within the fetish, bondage, domination, and submission (BDSM) community. It is perfectly expressed in "corset training" as part of the ritual within the dominant/submissive relationship. It is both a form of permanent bondage and constriction, a symbol of submission, and even of ownership whereby the person who ties the final knot takes control. Conversely, corsets also make people feel more in control of themselves, more confident, as they stand taller, untouchably encased in steel and impeccable craftsmanship, true goddesses to be worshipped.

The power of the corset

In modern times, when a dominant partner (usually female but not exclusively) dons a corset, she feels more authoritative, aloof, and untouchable. Her status becomes enhanced, while the lowly rank of the submissive is reinforced by the presence of ongoing corset training that insures that the "slave" is constantly reminded to whom he belongs. In this situation the corset becomes a tool of bondage and domination. It can also be used in cross-dressing, to feminize the male form; whether this is a privilege or a punishment is purely subjective. The fetish aspect of corset cross-dressing is also documented at length in *The Englishwoman's Domestic Magazine*. In numerous letters to the editor, the practice described in intricate detail and can be summarized as cruel ladies curbing the spirit of naughty boys by means of tightlacing.

The corset and personal fantasies

In the closing years of the 20th century the corset made a bold return to modern culture. Over the last 20 years it has allowed its wearers to express – among many different personas – their inner modern primitive, showgirl, romantic Goth or fetishist. Since the the dawn of psychoanalysis at the turn of the 20th century, the popularity of therapy, self-development and personal growth has grown in all areas of society, and personal exploration of our alternative personalities and archetypes has become more widely acceptable.

This self-reflective trend is itself reflected in fetish costume, where elements of extreme fantasy are drawn from authority figures: these include uniforms, role play, tattoos and body piercing, and a general a desire to become something other than the everyday self. A similar, more mundane desire has always been present in the heart of every devotee of fashion. As cultural attitudes towards fetishism and alternative sexuality have changed, elements of the same uniforms including skyscraper shoes, rubber, leather, tattoos, and body piercing have been used in advertising, movies and high fashion. Corsets are constantly transcending the limits of the fetishist wardrobe to find their way into avant-garde fashion and more recently filtering all the way down to the level of popular fashion. Strictly speaking, fetishism is perceived to be a largely male proclivity and it is undoubtedly the case that some degree of fetishism exists within the "normal" range of male sexual tastes and desires. Fetishism was defined academically for the first time by the Austro-German psychiatrist and sexologist Richard von Krafft Ebing in his 1886 book *Psychopathia Sexualis*, a series of case studies on the varied nature of human sexuality.

Objects of fetish

During the 19th century, with limited expression for sexual freedom and experimentation within "respectable" society, many men developed fetishes that focused on such items as feet, shoes, petticoats, gloves, silk, satin, velvet, furs, and corsets (these being the most common). According to the definition of fetishism, the list is potentially limitless. Fetishism is defined as a displacement of sexual desire onto an object or non-genital body part. This displacement of sexual desire may range from a slight preference for the object to be present for sexual arousal to occur, to the object itself being the sole focus of sexual gratification. The word fetish was originally used to describe an African amulet or charm imbued with magical powers, a sacred object of ritualist significance. The two meanings are highly apt for this category of unconventional and unusual sexual behaviour.

In the 19th century, the most desirable, cultivated and cherished female attributes were petite hands, small waists, and tiny feet, even long slender necks graced the growing menu of the Victorian gentleman's proclivities. The corset, with its ability to narrow and refine the body, was a part of the everyday ritual of dress for 19th-century women across all classes. Even the 19th-century male dandy may have worn corsets and many letters penned by "Walter" in the *The Englishwoman's Domestic Magazine*, suggest a possible subculture of male fetishists with erotic fantasies of tightlacing taking place in England's boarding schools.

For women, the actual evidence suggests that corsets were merely a practical part of their everyday dress and not generally tightly-laced. "Tightlacing" differs from the term "corseting" and the two should not be confused. Corseting is the practice of wearing a corset as an everyday item of clothing, to create light control and to help to align the body.

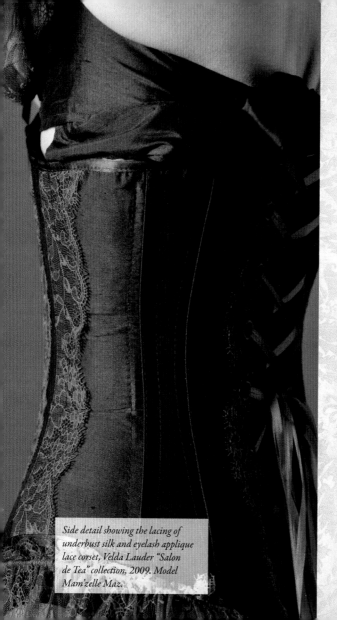

Ethel Granger and the tiny waist

The English tightlacer Ethel Granger entered *The Guinness Book of Records* with the smallest recorded tight-laced waist. Ethel began tightlacing in the 1920s, having brief periods of rest from lacing when she was pregnant and during World War ll but returning to her tiny 13-inch pre-war proportions in the 1950s. Ethel achieved a degree of fame and raised the profile of tightlacing during the late 1950s and 1960s. She died in 1982 having corseted for most of her life.

Side detail showing the lacing of underbust silk and eyelash applique lace corset, Velda Lauder "Salon de Tea" collection, 2009. Model Mam'zelle Maz.

The practice of tightlacing

Tightlacing is the extreme and continuous practice of lacing a corset to achieve an overtly tiny waist. The practice of tightlacing in the 19th century was actually surprisingly rare, most surviving corsets have measurements well within the normal range for women of the era. Reports of women with severe health issues as a result of extreme tightlacing are mostly dismissed today as thinly disguised misogyny, and the extreme reaction of certain social reformers. The Victorian era was rife with the fear of women's innate sexuality ironically, during this time the corset remained a object of sexual fantasy and focus. It was a time of sexual schizophrenia, with the corset central to the scene.

Corsets fell out of favor in the early 20th century, only emerging into the mainstream again with Christian Dior's New Look in the 1940s. In the 1950s strongly defined gender roles reappeared. The inflated bust was largely a post-war trend and women's fashions became ultra curvy. The balance of broad hips, ample bosoms, and a small waist are strongly associated with youth and fertility. As male sexual arousal is highly susceptible to visual cues, many men find small waists irresistible.

Because the corset articulates the waist by constricting the mid area, it displaces body mass elsewhere. There is a direct relationship between the reduction of the waist and increase in curvature of the hips and indeed the silhouette of the bust. The corset is able to make the proportional relationship of this secondary sexual characteristic more extreme in a way that is particularly pleasing to a man's eye.

John Willie and 1950s fetish imagery

With curvaceousness back at the heart of 1950s fashion consciousness, naughtiness appeared in the shape of John Willie who credited for bringing fetish imagery into the mainstream in the 1950s. Willie's imagination and distinctive graphic style introduced contemporary society to bondage, domination, and submission (BDSM) themes. He is particularly renowned for his fetish drawings of uber curvy women. From the late 1940s through to the late 1950s his character, "Sweet Gwendoline," and her tormentor "U69" appeared particularly tight-laced in Willie's *Bizarre* magazine.

Born John Alexander Scott Coutts in Singapore in 1902, Willie moved to New York to pursue his dream of becoming a bondage illustrator and artist. He is credited with influencing artists such as Eric Stanton and creating a genre of fetish illustration that is still popular today.

Cathie Jung

In the present day, the smallest recorded measurement for a tight-laced waist belongs to Cathie Jung who can lace down to 15 inches. Jung is an American who is married to an orthopaedic surgeon, who has consistently dismissed rumors that his wife has had an operation to remove a rib to achieve the desired reduction, stating the lower floating ribs are very flexible and can safely adapt to the effects of corseting.

Cathie has said that she corsets herself for her husband and it is his strong interest that keeps her going, but feels that hers is the attitude of an older generation of corset wearers, with younger female corset enthusiasts and fetishists indulging in tightlacing for their own, different reasons. Contemporary corseted women report an increasingly pleasant feeling of compression as they tighten the corset, describing a sensation that is akin to a long embrace. This pleasurable experience is one of the many reasons for their obsession with the corset.

The complexity of the corset seems to invite wearers into its long embrace, a tactile interaction that is entirely on the wearer's own terms. It holds you in as you stand taller, encased in steel, contoured and coutured, autonomous, and sexually in control. It is a garment for personal pleasure, potentially a dominatrix's armor, and a portal of personal control: all these are the modern woman's gifts from the corset.

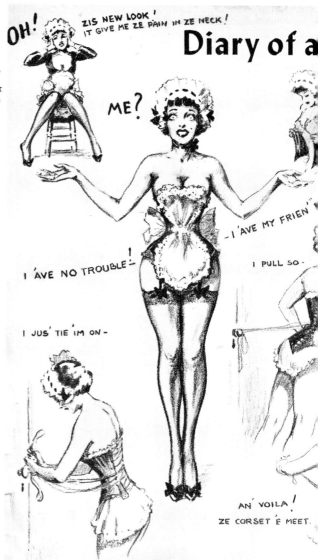

"The Diary of a French Maid," John Willie illustration in Flirt *magazine, published by Robert Harrison, December 1948 - February 1950.*

Thierry Mugler "Chimere" evening ensemble articulated with gold, feathers, scales, and hair, embroidered with jewels, Thierry Mugler "Couture" collection, fall/winter 1997.

Thierry Mugler and corset inspiration

Perhaps inspired by and undoubtedly incorporating the visual characteristics of John Willie's fantasy women, French designer Thierry Mugler has often portrayed his models as corset-clad superwomen, cartoon-like in their mighty stature, covered in chrome, leather, rubber and impeccable tailoring, the epitome of the modern uber-woman. Other designers have played with the corset in their own ways: Jean Paul Gaultier created a pink pointed bustier for Madonna (see page 76) while Alexander McQueen followed with a series of feminist fashion statements. Traditional fetishists at last had permission to step out of the closet; their corsets had been rubberiszed, buckled, and often totally reconstructed, but most importantly were now worn proudly worldwide.

The rubber revolution

The corset has always been a staple of the underground bondage scene, being as it were hardwired into the human mind, along with shoes, as the most common fetish item. Technical advances in the making of rubber transformed the material from an industrial textile into a fine second-skin fabric, allowing it to be used as a clothing material capable of incredible structure and creativity. It was time for the corset and rubber to come together.

Viktoria Modesta in rubber outfit, at Torture Garden, London, 2009.

New designs in rubber

In 1983 Skin Two appeared in London, the brainchild of Tim Woodward. Skin Two started in a cellar in Soho as an underground fetish club and was the initiator of the modern fetish club scene.

In 1984, Woodward, along with photographer Grace Lau founded *Skin Two* magazine alongside the Skin Two clothing range he was developing with Judy Wild. Skin Two eventually developed into a shop selling rubber fashions and associated glossy magazines that featured avant-garde photo-shoots of highly polished rubber creations, with the corset often central to the theme. Since its arrival *Skin Two* magazine has been a reference source for art directors and photographers, influencing contemporary movies and commercials, fashion magazines and, high fashion collections.

In the early 1990s the Dutch rubber company De Mask, based in Amsterdam, began to make rubber fetish clothing that focused on structured masks and corsets. Soon an army of small rubber clothing design companies appeared, primarily in the U.K., developing unique methods of working with this specialized material and pushing the boundaries of design and structure, with companies such as House of Harlot and Inner Sanctum focusing on rubber corsetry in particular.

Goth punk female reveler, London, 1990s.

Fetish imagery in the mainstream

This revolution has led to the appearance in mainstream culture of numerous fetishistic images and items. A perfect example is the dominatrix sky high stiletto shoe, until recently thought to be reserved solely for the bedroom. However, after high-profile appearances in various advertising campaigns, impossibly high shiny five-inch heels appeared on Paris catwalks, and today the most popular chain stores emulate the same dizzy heights with skyscraper heels trimmed with fake petite, metallic padlocks. Bondage straps and corsets followed as common themes on the catwalk and in the 21st century they too are filtering down to the high street en-masse. Wasp-waisted buckled belts are common fashion trends while wet look fabrics are replacing vintage rubber leggings in Main Street shops and on the catwalk.

Vivienne Westwood and Malcolm McLaren were style leaders in the 1970s punk scene. McLaren's subversive attitude and Westwood's obsession with historical detail and references, led her to thoroughly research the clandestine world of London's BDSM scene and engage designers from this community to manufacture some of her items. Unique and outlandish at the time, these creations were sold in Westwood and McLaren's shop "SEX" at World's End on London's Kings Road.

Many of the early collections incorporated strong elements of classic bondage and domination paraphernalia. Westwood introduced, and eventually fully integrated, the overtly shocking and sexual into the world of mainstream fashion. When punks in the King's Road began to wear

Fakir Musafer, "The perfect Gentleman, 1959."

elements of the uniform of the dominatrix, the fetishist secret was on display for all to see and admire.

The modern primitive

My own fascination with the corset developed rapidly when I moved to London in the early 1990s. London was in the grip of its latest subcultural revolution which would eventually impact on the rest of the world, and as the Goth scene waned, the "modern primitives" were emerging. For them, the body itself became the canvas for self-expression, from body modification rituals, to decorative body piercing and tattooing. Corset training once more gained a place within an emerging western culture. The modern primitives were exponents of multiple and conspicuous piercing, tribal tattooing, and even branding and scarification as permanent emblems of the scene. Corsets and their tremendous ability to mould the physique, became a key part of their arsenal of body modifications.

The father of the modern primitive movement is Fakir Musafer. Born Roland Loomis in the U.S.A in 1930, he began at the age of 12 to modify his body with self-piercing. Later he explored using his body as an instrument of western contemporary shamanism through a series of ritualized body modification practices. He is the subject of numerous movies and television documentaries and travels the world as a speaker on new age shamanism, promoting the concept of the modern primitive.

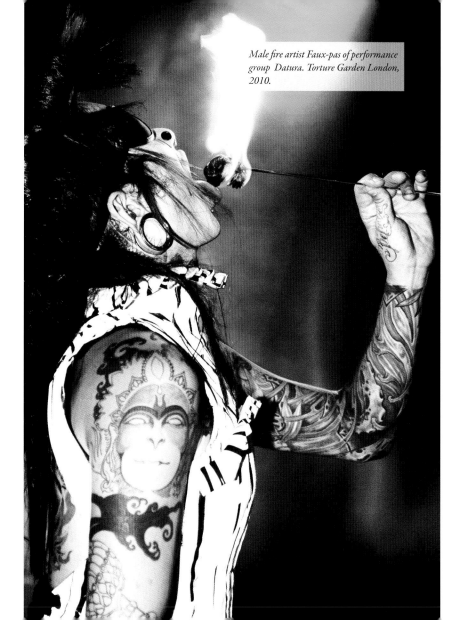

Male fire artist Faux-pas of performance group Datura. Torture Garden London, 2010.

Modern primitives and the corset

Musafer's great passion for the corset and his personal corseting practice has been an inspiration for the master corsetière Mr. Pearl. Indeed, Fakir Musafer was known as the "Ol' Corsetiere." One of his most famous photos, "the perfect gentleman" (see page 136) shows him tight-laced but wearing shirt and tie, flawlessly presented as a modern dandy. The comparison with later photos of Mr. Pearl are clear (see page 156). Musafer used the corset as part of his body modification apparatus, and the unfolding modern primitive society followed.

The new desire for modern urban tribal initiation began with a few pockets of subversive individuals and has grown into the widespread modern trend for navel, nose, genital, and multiple ear piercings, alongside a range of tattoos and the use of the corset as a fashion staple. Both piercing and tattooing saw a boom in business in the late 20th century.

The Torture Garden

As the fetishists came out of the closet, the early 1990s Goth scene fused with the growing body arts scene. All wrapped up in exciting newly liberated rubber fabrics, the new breed of modern primitive was ready for the birth of the Torture Garden in London. Radical high-end fashion statements from Westwood and Gaultier, in conjunction with the art

Reveler in a crown and mask, Torture Garden London, 2010.

house images of *Skin Two* magazine contributed to fetish fashion and creativity entering the mainstream. The Torture Garden's unique mixture of progressive music, fashion, performance, and visuals created a platform for a new era of cultural expression and fusion. The Torture Garden has been extensively featured in movies and television as well as the mainstream press, and is now the biggest fetish club in the world, hosting events in Paris, Moscow, Tokyo, New York, Los Angeles, and Berlin. The burlesque specialist Dita von Teese made her U.K. performance debut at Torture Garden in 1999.

As my first corset collections were regularly purchased by Torture Garden devotees (from fashionistas to tightlacers), I was privileged to experience from within the dawn of a new era. The finest corsetières and alternative fashion designers in the world present their collections in spectacular shows on the Torture Garden's stage to great approval and enthusiasm.

Antique pink glitter and lace underbust corset, Velda Lauder, 2009. Model Koneko.

The corset as High Fashion

Christian Dior's New Look of 1947 incorporated corsets as a major structural feature of a garment, necessary to produce the desired shape. His fellow couturier Jacques Fath featured intricate boning in the bodices of his evening gowns. Both were an inspiration to the high fashion designers of the 1980s and later. From Vivienne Westwood's classic interpretations of the corset, to Jean Paul Gaultier, Thierry Mugler, and Alexander McQueen's futuristic creations and the more classical inspirations of John Galliano and Christian Lacroix, a whole generation has once again been entranced by the corset, assuring it a key role in the pantheon of modern fashion.

Christian Dior fitting a model into one of his New Look creations, circa 1950.

COUTURE GARMENTS are exclusive, custom-fitted clothing designed by couturiers, traditionally hand made by skilled seamstresses using specialist techniques and the finest quality materials and fabrics. Couture corsets recaptured the catwalk in 1947 with Christian Dior's New Look. Dior's triumphant collection instantly inspired this comment from American *Vogue's* fashion editor, Bettina Ballard: "I was conscious of the electric tension I had never before felt in couture...We were witnesses to a revolution in fashion." After the austerity of wartime rationing, clothes coupons and military uniforms, the feminine figure was back in fashion. *L'Express* wrote of Christian Dior that he was, "unknown on the 12th of February 1947, famous on the 13th."

Dior encouraged his models to use the structure and the volume of the fabric in his skirts as they moved. With his direction, his models swished and sashayed through the salons, creating a sensation and reviving a desire for exuberance and a triumphant return to femininity. Dior reintroduced the handspan waist, emphasized by full skirts and padded hips, the voluptuous female forming the foundation for his signature silhouette. The New Look silhouette was created by the use of traditional corsetry, waspies, and underpinnings with corsetry both built into the pieces themselves and as separate undergarments. Although Charles Frederick Worth is regarded as the father of couture in post-war Paris, Christian Dior and his New Look were seen as the very salvation of couture.

White back-laced bodice bustier, lace petticoat and black lace topped stockings from the Jacques Fath collection, 1954.

"Botte Secrete" evening gown, "des robes qui se derobent," Jean Paul Gaultier "Haute Couture" collection spring/ summer, 2001.

Jacques Fath and the Gaultier influence

During this New Look period Jacques Fath introduced heavily boned bustiers into his glamorous evening gown collections, launching the concept of corsetry as outerwear. His use of the traditional foundation garment hue of shell pink in many of his boned gowns evokes the effect of intimate apparel as elegant evening wear.

Although between the 1950s and 1990s corsets were rarely seen on the catwalk, the influence of the 1940s designs continues to reverberate down the decades. Echoes of Jacques Fath's work can be seen in John Paul Gaultier's haute couture girdle dresses and his frequent use of classic lingerie shades of peach and pink. Gaultier's "Botte Secrete Evening Gown" from his spring/summer 2001 haute couture collection uses classic back corset lacing to emphasize the tension in the garment, with the lacing extending the full length of the dress, and the long satin ribbon flowing from the knees into a elongated train of cascading streamers.

Christian Lacroix's new Belle Epoque

In the mid-1990s Christian Lacroix reintroduced corsets to the couture catwalk when he created sumptuous silk corsets inspired by the late 19th-century Belle Epoque era. Delicate layers of uber feminine silk formed bustles and bows, further exaggerating the curve of a cinched-in waist and heralding the return of the corset as a catwalk centerpiece. Throughout

Underwear as outerwear

"Dita Von Teese and the burlesque movement inspired John Galliano's show of '40s showgirls, which in turn encouraged the high street to kit us out in underwear as outerwear."
Kay Barron, Grazia, *January 2010.*

"Saks Fifth Avenue announce the corselette has emerged as the ultimate accessory."
New York Times, *August, 1994.*

"Fashion's erogenous zone has shifted to the waist."
British Vogue, April, 2001.

Pop star and singer Kylie Minogue performs on the opening night of her North American Tour, dressed in Jean Paul Gaultier outfit, 2009.

the 1990s the corset was embraced with renewed passion by designers as diverse as Azzedine Alaia, Karl Lagerfeld, Versace, and Valentino, who incorporated this versatile garment into their catwalk collections.

The subversion of Jean Paul Gaultier

While Vivienne Westwood and Christian Lacroix evoked the Belle Epoch and classic 18th-century shapes for their vision, Thierry Mugler and Jean Paul Gaultier looked to the future for inspiration. The 20th-century postmodern trend for traditional lingerie worn as outerwear is perhaps best seen in Jean Paul Gaultier's work. Born on 24 April, 1952, in Arcueil Val-de-Marne, France, Gaultier's introduction and fascination with the corset is credited to his grandmother's influence, although his corset-clad creatures are pure cartoon, futurist and fetishist.

Gaultier's exaggeration of body parts and use of current subcultural themes make him one of the most unorthodox designers of the 20th century. Pierced, tattooed, and skirted men come to life on his catwalks, subverting the traditional gender roles and conjuring up scenes from post-apocalyptic sci-fi movies. Gaultier had no formal training as a designer, and his anarchic edge is often inspired directly by street culture. His irreverent style earned him the title "enfant terrible." Gaultier's futuristic style is exemplified in the costumes he created for Luc Besson's movie the *Fifth Element.*

Thierry Mugler "Robot Couture" silver cyborg suit, silver metal and plexiglas, fall/winter collection, 1995.

Thierry Mugler and the noir goddess

Thierry Mugler's world is filled with viragos encased in impeccable tailoring: clean cut and towering, sexy yet scary, the strict shapes and curves accentuate the female form. Mugler's woman could be described as a fusion of a John Willie cartoon (see pages 126–129) and a comic book superhero, with the corset always at the center of the story. Mugler's audacious architectural style originated with his original training as a ballet dancer. Here he gained a sense of the theatrical and the esthetics of the body that he would later use to produce his magnificent catwalk shows, videos, and collaborations with Cirque du Soleil.

Mugler's first women's collection was launched in Paris in 1973, with menswear and haute couture collections following. Initially his inspiration came from the screen goddesses of the *film noir* genre, but his motorcycle corset dress and robot corset encasements made in plexiglass and metal, are entirely items of futuristic fantasy. His unique signature style quickly established his ability to merge fashion, fantasy, and fetishistic elements. This is exemplified in his exoskeletal leather insect inspired collection: the collection portrays science fiction mutants where the model merges with the leather layered corset, to create images of a dark world of arachnids, insect armor, the dark goddess and the wicked witch of fairy tales. Mugler has used controversial fabrics such as PVC, rubber, plexiglass, and metal to sculpt the female form with magnificent effect, bringing us into his tightly corseted world of "glamazons" in techno fabrics. Mugler's singular vision has inspired many of the the current generation of corsetières and designers such as Alexander McQueen, Gareth Pugh and Velda Lauder.

Alexander McQueen "Silver Coil Corset" worn with grey wool puffball skirt and skating shoes, "The Overlook" collection, fall /winter 2000.

Alexander McQueen, the perfectionist rebel

In his too short life, Alexander McQueen added a sense of fantasy and rebellion to the fashion world. With his uncompromising ideas and irreverent attitude he was sometimes regarded as the hooligan of British fashion and an industry anarchist. But he was critically acclaimed in equal measure, winning the British Designer of the Year award four times, International Designer of the Year and a CBE in 2003. McQueen's intensive training in tailoring and his profound respect for fine workmanship, plus his incorporation of artisan crafts, enabled him to produce the most exquisite and exciting clothing, and he very quickly became one of the most respected designers in the world.

McQueen's shows were legendary; he projected a complex image of women as strong yet vulnerable, triumphant yet tortured. His inspiration sprang from his sometimes macabre observations of women's experiences; his genius often fueled by his own dark subconscious. McQueen's corsetry, molded and sometimes almost orthopedic in structure, is the opposite of the traditionally feminine or classically erotic. In the world of McQueen the corset often becomes a woman's brace, to prop up, fix or protect her from injury. While Thierry Mugler's women are dark goddesses incapsulating powerful erotic energy, Alexander McQueen's statuesque tailored models show a more sinister side; his themes are the antithesis of Mugler's "glamazons." McQueen's women are bloodied and bound, the corset is their armor against a cruel modern world.

Mr. Pearl, New York City, 1993.
Photograph by Michael James
O'Brien.

Mr. Pearl and the gentleman's corset

Mr. Pearl is without doubt the most famous corsetière in the world. He is himself a genuine tightlacer, famous for wearing his corset constantly, precisely pruning and pinching his body like the gradual grooming of a treasured Japanese bonsai, resulting in a waist reduction to 18 inches. His unique silhouette strikes a fascinating if slightly disturbing note, insuring a delicate demeanour, the ultimate projection of the perfect gentlemen. The corset has transformed his waist into the pivotal point of a wasp, evoking images of Thierry Mugler's "Carapace."

Mr. Pearl has formed a deep relationship with his corset and the associated demands of achieving and maintaining a minute midriff. He is passionate about corsets, his obsession resulting in his self-taught skill as a corsetière. He credits strict self-discipline and self-control with the achievement of his incredible waist reduction, and his devotion has rewarded him with his extraordinary waist and an illustrious couture client list. He has created exquisite corsets for the collections of Christian Lacroix, Thierry Mugler, Vivienne Westwood, Jean Paul Gaultier and John Galliano. Celebrity devotees include Dead or Alive star Pete Burns, Kylie Minogue, Victoria Beckham, and Dita Von Teese.

Dior "High Fashion" collection spring/summer, 2010 by John Galliano.

Galliano, the great fashion seducer

In complete contrast to Alexander McQueen, with his iconoclastic creations, fellow Londoner John Galliano identifies his love of theater, historical research, and femininity as his main influences and inspiration. He has been quoted as saying simply that "my role is to seduce." Galliano's collections are flamboyant and romantic, a timeless vision of femininity, a fantasy.

Galliano moved from Givenchy to Christian Dior in 1997 just in time for the 50th anniversary of the launch of the New Look. His love of research and detail insured a spectacular return to the essential essence of the House of Dior. The first British designer to be appointed as head of a couture house since Charles Worth, Galliano revitalized Parisian couture. Although *Queen* magazine had proclaimed the death of couture as long ago as 1946, with his heightened sense of elegance and femininity, couture was reborn with John Galliano in 1997.

Galliano's love of the elegant creations of Christian Dior and Jacques Fath can be seen in his reccurring use of the classic nipped-in waist and built-up hips of the early Dior New Look collections. Galliano has worked consistently with corsetière Mr. Pearl, to create the most spectacularly embellished corsetry.

The full splendor, artistry, and technical skill of the Parisian couture houses is superbly utilized in order to bead, lace and appliqué the garments; the corsets cut and tight-laced to fainting level by the

Transparent guipiere and skirt of crinkled plastic, Chanel spring/summer "Haute Couture" collection, 1993, by Karl Lagerfeld, modeled by Claudia Schiffer.

virtuosity of Mr. Pearl. This level of corset reduction and definition had not been seen since the early 20th century. With the collaboration of the two maestros Galliano and Pearl, the opulence and beauty of the corset reached a zenith of creative expression and craftsmanship. Galliano's 2010 menswear collection saw the corset adorning the male torso, with echoes of both Mr. Pearl's infamous 1994 photograph "The Perfect Gentleman" and an earlier, but similarly shirted and corseted image of Fakir Musafer. Although the corseted gentleman remains rare, his influence is strong, as witnessed by Karl Lagerfeld's photographs of his male muse, Baptiste Giabiconi, and in a Velda Lauder underbust buckle corset that featured in *Purple* magazine in November 2009.

Corsets as everyday outerwear

Karl Lagerfeld's 1983 appointment as head of the house of Chanel saw him insisting on structure as a base for his new body-hugging designs. A series of sensational corsets followed. Lagerfeld has consistently used shiny fetish imagery in his collections for Chanel, Fendi, and his own Karl Lagerfeld label, inspiring designers such as Dolce and Gabbana and Gucci to follow his lead with buckled bustiers and monochromatic boned dresses.

Stella McCartney teamed her corsets with suits to create a clean tailored line with the corset clearly defined as daywear, a commentary on the

Model Lauren Ridealgh wearing
Velda Lauder "Peace Warrior"
collection, 2007.

power dressing of the materialistic 1980s, which is also referenced in Thierry Mugler's clean-cut triangular silhouette and patternless blocked colored women's suits.

The underbust corset

In 2005 Velda Lauder launched her "Peace Warrior" collection, inspired by the nostalgic tailoring, colors and themes of post-war Britain, and from this collection emerged the short, buckled underbust corset. The introduction of a simple underbust variant further popularized the corset to make it a basic component of daywear. This innovation has made the corset extremely wearable and versatile, with this particular design delivering maximum curve control with comfort while being reproduced in more conventional fabrics such as denim, cotton drill, and classic pinstripes. The Velda Lauder "Dita" corset design (see page 106), which fuses classic 1940s tailoring with 21st-century sophistication, redefines the role of the corset creating a versatile piece that can be dressed up for evening wear, coordinated with girdles or French knickers for the boudoir, or worn with a classic jacket and skirt for everyday wear.

The corset on the catwalk

The corset has become a integral part of the fashion world at all levels, with abstract aspects of its various components appearing as details on casual garments from sportswear to daywear. Lacing, eyelets, stitching, and boning are now used to suggest an illusion of corseting, exemplified in the collections of Yves Saint Laurent, Balenciaga, Comme des Garçons, and Jean Paul Gaultier.

Alexander McQueen's "Pluto's Atlantis" collection for spring/summer 2010 delivers clever curves that are precision cut to create futuristic forms and shapes, space age in tone yet directly descended from Dior's New Look. *Vogue's* 1994 prediction seems to have come true: "take a deep breath, a style made popular by Christian Dior ... in 1947 is back."

Corsetry has become a regular participant in the fashion arena. Its longevity lies in its ability to adapt to different surroundings and changing environments. Its durability stems from its essential strength of design, utility, and flexibility; the garment develops and evolves with the times. The corset's design cousins – basques, bustiers, merry widows, girdles, waspies, and modern contour shapewear – all sculpt and enhance the human form.

The importance of technology

Technological breakthroughs in the development of stretch fibers and materials have led to significant advances in shapewear in recent years, with lighter, stronger materials allowing the body to breathe and stay cool and free of perspiration. Anatomical molding has allowed body-enhancing contour garments to add to the overall effect, selectively increasing the bust and lifting the buttocks. Power mesh, Lycra, Spandex, light rubber, and nylon are layered to create varying levels of control, the compression capabilities of the materials considerably slimming the waist and thigh areas.

The popularity of the new era of contour garments can be seen in frequent references to the brand Spanx; even on the red carpet on Oscar night, actresses refer to wearing their Spanx under their couture gowns. On television, contour garments are an essential tool in the armory of the makeover artist; the idea that you can look five years younger and become three inches smaller, all over, instantly explains the popularity of Spanx, Vedette, Squeem, Esbelt, Rago, and a multitude of new body control brands. Hosiery, joined the contour collective with tights promising tummy and thigh control and hold ups reinforced with Lycra and shimmering glass effects, creating luminous, long, lean legs.

Lilly Cole models an Agent Provocateur underwear set, Life Ball Vienna, 2008.

A return to glamorous undies

The burlesque revival of the late 1990s has seen a resurgence in vintage lingerie, with a return to fifties Hollywood glamor and forties elegant styles. A new and exciting wave of British lingerie designers began to appear at this time. In 1994 Joe Corré (son of Malcolm McLaren and Vivienne Westwood) and Serena Rees created Agent Provocateur as an antidote to the lack of appealing underwear for British women. The label fused fine quality with quintessential cheeky British chic, and classic lingerie became once more sexy and contemporary. The Agent Provocateur look inspires confidence and desire in both the observer and the observed and the impeccable credentials and eye for design created an instant celebrity following and successful business, with more than 30 Agent Provocateur shops in 14 countries worldwide. Agent Provocateur opened the doors to a new era in lingerie design, with their unique fusion of fun and sophistication. British lingerie suddenly became big business.

In 2001 Sam Roddick opened Coco de Mer in Covent Garden which showcased a unique selection of sexy avant-garde objets d'art and limited edition lingerie. Almost instantly, a number of small, vintage-inspired lingerie companies sprang up to produce a wave of British innovation and creativity in contour, sexy and vintage underwear as outerwear and outerwear as underwear. "What Katie Did," "Made by Nikki," "Kiss me Deadly" and the "Velda Lauder's Corset Compliments" collection are all notable retro inspired design companies. The trend has filtered from the catwalk to the shopping mall, with bustiers, basques, bodices, and corsets making a dramatic impression everywhere you look.

Model Mam'zelle Maz wears classic long-line, demi-cup corset in silk and eyelash lace, Velda Lauder "Salon de Tea" collection, 2009.

Model Bex Paul wears soft mesh hanky bra, short satin bow-front underbust corset, mesh bloomers and gloves. Velda Lauder "Gothikka" collection, 2010.

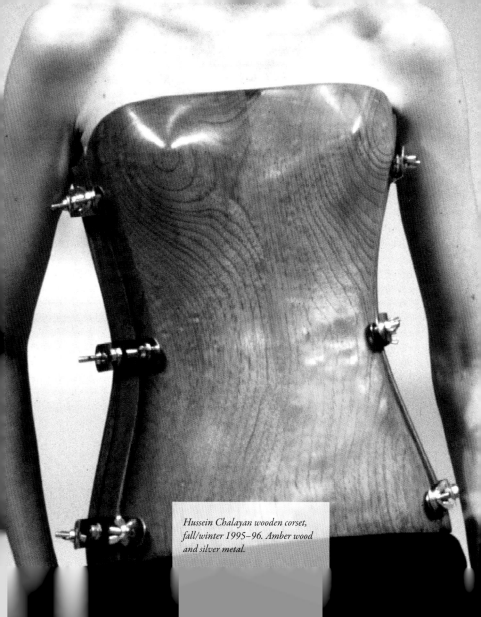

Hussein Chalayan wooden corset, fall/winter 1995–96. Amber wood and silver metal.

Variations on the Classic Corset

In recent years the corset has provided an ideal base on which designers can create art as opposed to mere fashion. Inspiration has come from many quarters: John Galliano at Dior with the beaded corsets of the Dinka of East Africa; Alexander McQueen with the structure of the human body itself. The remarkable Issey Miyake looked to Japanese traditional dress and the armour of Samurai warriors for his influences as did his compatriot, Junko Koshino. Very recently, the performance artist Lady Gaga has used her own body as a canvas, with the corset at the heart of her persona.

Thierry Mugler "Carapace Couture" collection spring/summer, 1997. Shell carved leather sheath and skirt finged with black feathers.

The corset as art

As women became more health conscious during the 1980s, they began to transform their bodies using exercise, diet, and cosmetic surgery rather than corsetry and other artificial means. At the same time, the corset began to take on a new role, that of an object of high art. The hard canvas of the corset became the blank sheet for creative expression of a generation of designers in the late 20th century. Designers such as Thierry Mugler, Issey Miyake, Alexander McQueen and John Galliano simultaneously seem to have found inspiration within the insect world, the whole range of arthropoda influencing numerous and varied collections.

A gorgeous carapace

The firm, shell-like structure of the corset provides an ideal hard surface on which to express the fantasies of the designer. Moving beyond its traditional role of support and body sculpting, the corset became the work of art itself. Much conventional lingerie has a delicate quality, whereas corsetry exudes power while protecting the body. The creators of these new corsets expressed a sense of power with their choice of materials: shiny surfaces were rendered in chrome, gloss-finished fiberglass and rubber, complemented by wood, plaster, and leather. The impression created was one of armored impenetrability as the model wearing the garment became a living sculpture.

Issey Miyake designed molded red plastic "Bustier," corset 1980.

Thierry Mugler "Harley Davidson" bustier, plexiglas, hand-painted on black leather shorts, quilted heart in the back and fringed red leather, spring/summer "Motorcycle" collection, 1992.

Lady Gaga attends the 2010 Grammy Awards, wearing a Giorgio Armani creation, the "Prive corset dress."

Robot women

Thierry Mugler's "Robot Couture" show of fall/winter 1995, may have been inspired by the artwork of the Japanese artist Hajime Sorayama. In this collection Mugler encased the model's body in plexiglass and chrome, she became a futuristic vision, an intergalactic cybernetic dominatrix (see page 152). In the *New York Times* Mugler was quoted as saying, "I used to be accused of not liking women, but in truth I invented a very efficient silhouette, a body-conscious look that was both modern and very flattering."

Mugler's hard bodied creations mirrored Japanese designer Issey Miyake's molded fiberglass breastplates, with Mugler building on Miyake's theme with his 1992 "Motorcycle" collection (see pages 174-5). Mugler's "robot woman" and "motorcycle" designs were reworked and recreated as costumes for the singer Beyonce's 2010 tour. Mugler's distinctive style is once more in demand with the recent trend for Metal Couture, as cyborg styling has become a flourishing 21st-century trend. Manuel Albarran's beautiful metal corsets and head pieces perfectly complement the Mugler's creations, while Giorgio Armani's Prive corset dress as worn by Lady Gaga, is a perfect example of wearable art

Alexander McQueen molded bodice,
part of the spring/summer collection,
1999.

Surgical corset made from leather and
metal, designed by Hussein Chalayan,
1998.

Asymmetrical, textured leather, flame-pointed corset, worn by Marisa Millar. Created by Velda Lauder for Victoria's Secret, 2008.

Mirroring the body

In complete contrast, Alexander McQueen's leather corset designed for Givenchy for fall/winter 1999, contrasts the organic softness of the inner flesh with the external hardness of the materials that are used to form the torso. This sculptural piece features fully formed breasts, a belly button and clavicle in molded leather. Painted deep blood red as if the skin has been peeled away to reveal the flesh below, it is a striking, thought-provoking piece. McQueen took the effect further with his "Prosthetic" corset of 1999, here the "flesh" of the piece was "sutured" to further disturb and provoke.

Hussein Chalayan's "Surgical corset" designed in 1998 suggests a remedial function. All of its boning, strapping, and supports are on show and the corset becomes a mechanical brace to hold together an injured body. From Mugler's indestructible superheroines, to Chalayan's broken dolls, these uniquely crafted pieces can stand alone as sculptural installations that provoke discourse and debate, or they can be integrated into a futuristic wardrobe.

Traditional tribal costumes and corsets

The genius of John Galliano flourished when he was appointed as head of the house of Dior. His first collections exemplified his anachronistic brilliance, his ability to draw inspiration from both historical silhouettes and the tribal costumes of indigenous cultures. Queen Alexandra, wife of King Edward VII, the traditional attire of the Dinka warriors of the Sudan, the neck coils and neck rings of the Pedaung peoples of Burma and Thailand, and the Ndebele tribes of South Africa, were evident influences in Galliano's collections, reflected in his high jeweled necklaces, chokers and corsets.

It is said that Queen Alexandra wore her jewelled chokers to hide a scar, but her style was much admired and copied during the reign of her husband. Her influential high necklaces created a graceful long neckline and framework for her décolletage. Despite the huge historical and cultural differences, the similarity with the line of the Dinka warriors beaded neck corsets is unmissable. Karl Lagerfeld's personal style of black suit and starched high collar is reminiscent of both the rigidly elevated collars of the Edwardian era, and the proud elevated heads of the Ndebele culture. His signature style is included in the high collars and turtle necks on the catwalk for his Chanel fall/winter 2010 show.

The Dinka and their corsets

The statuesque Dinka tribe, who inhabit the Bahr el Ghazal region of the Nile basin, are credited with establishing cattle husbandry in southern Sudan. Cattle play a crucial part in their society, so much so that their flesh is rarely eaten. The Dinka see their cattle as an important link with

Dinka Girls eligible for marriage dressed in loose bead bodices of patterns which indicate family prosperity, how many cattle will be required as dowry, and cowrie shells to promote fertility. Sudan, 1998.

Dinka inspired ensemble, beaded hat, collar necklace and corset over a black satin dress with floral print train, shown in the Christian Dior spring/ summer "Couture" collection by John Galliano, 1997.

Issey Miyake fall/winter "Ready to Wear" collection by Naoki Takizawa, 2006.

the spiritual world, and the quantity of cattle owned by individuals is a symbol of their status.

To a Dinka man the importance of his corset comes second only to his cattle. The corsets are made from long strings of tiny colored beads placed in bands of colour horizontally around the body. The beads are attached to a strong central spine at the back, the spine often extending out from the body and its height denoting status and the number of cattle owned. At puberty, a Dinka man is sewn into his corset. The color of the corset denotes a particular age group, with a new color combination indicating the passage through the various life cycles until marriage, when the corset is usually ritualistically removed.

The Dinka corset is not just as an artistic expression or body adornment, it is also used to communicate the tribal affiliation, age, wealth, and gender of the wearer. Corsets are worn by both genders: The female corset is often a little looser than the male variant, and is called "Alual"; the male version is worn very tight and called "Maual." Today the Dinka people are facing huge problems resulting from wars ravishing their country, and many are now refugees. However, the wearing of the corset is so entrenched in their culture that in the absence of the treasured glass beads used to construct the corset, woolen versions are often made and worn to express ethnicity.

Corsets have also been worn by the tribesmen of Papua New Guinea. The youth of the tribe undergo a rite of passage at puberty. A wide belt made from bark, snake, or animal skin is beaten, stretched and lengthened, then wrapped tightly round the "Ibitoe" (initiate's) waist. The belt is known as an "Itaburi" and is tightened frequently to reduce the waist over time, as the smaller the waist, the higher his status in the community. Today the tightlacing is practised mostly for short periods of time rather than continuously, but remains an integral part of the culture. The founder of the modern primitive movement, Fakir Musafar, is very much influenced by the tightlacing practices of the Papua New Guinean "Ibitoe."

Corseting the neck

As well as their body corsets, the Dinka wear neck corsets, with a similar central core that creates the stunning visual effect of elongating the neck deep down into the chest and high up into the cranium. The similarity in shape to leather fetish neck corsets of the late 20th century and Queen Alexandra's early 20th-century jewels is undeniable. Beautiful, Dinka-inspired corsets, perfectly recreated by John Galliano for Christian Dior's haute couture collection for spring/summer 1997, mirror the majesty and magnificence of the original indigenous creations.

The Padaung people of the mountain area between Burma and Thailand wear heavy, coiled brass neck rings which create an unusual and somewhat surreal appearance. The long slender stalk-like effect is achieved by placing the first coils on the necks of female children at about five years

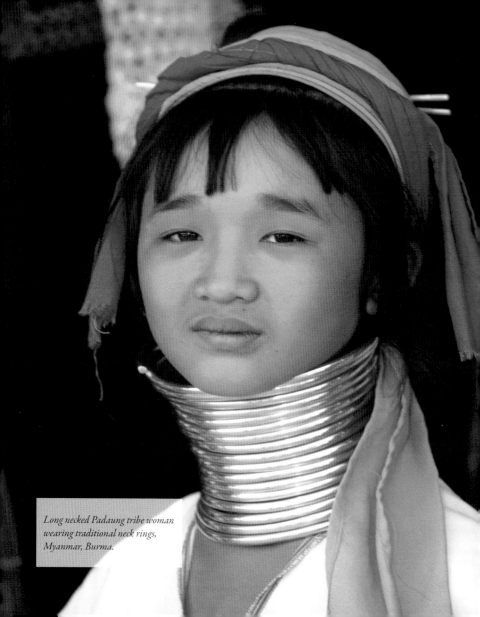

Long necked Padaung tribe woman wearing traditional neck rings, Myanmar, Burma.

of age. This first coil is replaced by longer and heavier coils as the child grows. The long neck appearance is actually achieved by pushing down the clavicle and shoulders with the weight of the rings, since the vertebrae of the neck cannot stretch.

This elongated effect is associated with tribal beauty and cultural identity. Wearing of the neck coils helps to promote marriages within the tribe's ethnic group. Various other theories of the significance of the neck coils have been put forward, for example that the coils help to protect against tiger bites and deter enslavement of the women during tribal warfare. Coils are also worn to a lesser extent around the knees, ankles, and wrists. These coils can be removed without major injury, with the body regaining its strength with time. With modern culture encroaching on the tribal identity of the Padaung people, some women are choosing not to wear the corset coils, with others seeing them simply as a way to attract tourists.

A similar custom is very much alive among the Ndebele women of South Africa, whose neck adornments are actually individual rings rather than coils. Upon marriage the rings replace the elaborate, dense, and wide bolsters that are used to prepare the neck for the heavy rings, as the rings can weigh up to four pounds each. Within the Ndebele culture the rings symbolize the marital bond and the wealth of the husband.

Fashion neck coil, Givenchy "Haute Couture" collection, fall/winter, 1997.

Interpreting the tribal

John Galliano specifically integrated this tribal neck coil imagery into his couture collection for Christian Dior for fall/winter 1997. The model Stella Tennant wore an elegant, elongated silver neck coil with a wasp-waisted gray suit. In the same year Thierry Mugler stacked bands of leather together to create a neck corset for his leather "Carapace" design (see page 172). At Givenchy, Alexander McQueen also used stacked neck rings as accessories in his couture collection in the same year and his silver coil corset from the "Overlook" collection, fall/winter 1999 (see page 154), extended the metal neck rings and coiled them downward to cover the whole torso and shoulders.

Japanese traditional dress and the waist

The sash worn around the waist of the traditional Japanese kimono is known as an obi. The type of obi varies with the wearer's status and gender and can be up to 20 yards in length. The long fabric is firmly bound around the wearer's waist and finished with a elaborate "Musubi" or knot. Again, the type of knot conveys a message about the wearer's status, or the event or celebration they are attending.

The interesting difference between an obi and a corset is that although the focus is still very much on the waistline, through the layering of fabric the obi actually builds up the waist rather than reducing it, and creating curvature. The addition of an obi board has a similar effect on the wearer to that of an old fashioned spoon busk, further curtailing the movement of the waist and insuring the only movement can be a low, straight bow from the hips.

From the 1970s onwards, innovative Japanese design pushed forward the boundaries of fabric and textile technologies, fusing novel Japanese techniques with unconventional materials. Many of the star designers integrated their experience of western culture with shapes and styles of traditional Japanese design, giving unexpected and exciting results

Issey Miyake, an artist in cloth

Issey Miyake, the master of modern textile techniques, studied and worked in Paris and New York before opening his first retail outlet in Japan. His understanding of Japanese form and shape, combined with the knowledge gained from his European and American experiences, led him to adopt a very different approach to design. He created two revolutionary new products: "Pleats Please" and "A-POC (A Piece of Cloth)."

"Pleats Please" was an incredible innovation in clothing. A garment was cut several sizes larger than the desired final size, then tiny pleats were sealed into the cloth to reduce the garment to the required size. The result allowed for a graceful interplay between the wearer and the garment.

"A-POC" introduced the concept of self-tailored clothing, as each piece could be individualized by the wearer. Computer programmed, industrial knitting machines produced tubes of fabric that the wearer could customize to the length and style they required. It is a form of interactive clothing that allows the client to partake in the design process and control the form of the final garment. Miyake's clothes synthesized avant-garde concepts and techniques with Japanese simplicity and harmony.

Miyake and the corset

In the early 1980s Miyake's unique take on the corset brought sculptural clothing to the forefront of the fashion world. In 1980 he created his legendary fiberglass red corset, a rigid vermillion bodice which contoured the breasts with flared peplum (see page 174), it became an instantly recognizable and iconic piece of sculpture. With this groundbreaking piece Issey Miyake had introduced the concept of the hard corset and suggested that it could act as a kind of haute couture armor.

Miyake also coupled sculptural materials with the traditional Japanese shapes of the Samurai's *kataginu,* the upper part of the Samurai formal dress, or *kamishimo*, resembling a sleeveless jacket with oversized pointed shoulders. For Miyake's 1982 spring/summer collection he sculpted a *kataginu* in lacquered bamboo. This *kataginu* had exaggerated winged shoulders which dramatically disappeared into a narrow molded waist.

*Atsuko Kudo, red corset dress.
modeled by Eden Berlin.*

Worn with full pleated *hakama* (the long trousers traditionally worn by Samurai), the exoskeletal effect of the winged shoulders is further emphasized by a sculpted armored waist.

In 1983 Miyake continued this distinctive exoskeletal style with his "wire bustier," an aluminum wire "cuff corset" which snapped around the torso and encased the body as if it were a bird in a cage. Miyake went on to introduce zipped silicone bustiers in his 1985 fall/winter collection; these were accessorized with huge polyurethane trousers with inflatable hips. These cartoon-like trousers appeared to dramatically diminish the size of the waist; a corseted caricature image of the uber woman had come to life.

Other Japanese designers and the corset

While a generation of Japanese designers developed monochromatic, loose comfortable clothing, others followed Issey Miyake's sculptural corset trend. In 1991 Yoshiki Hishinuma recreated the neck corset with his solid shiny plexiglass collars to complement his textural body sculptured creations. Echoes of Issey Miyake's exoskeletal *kataginu* corset and wire bustier are evident in Junko Koshino's 1992 "bustier in synthetic codes ensemble." Architectural in shape, it has a bone-white skeletal corset that floats over a black body suit, creating space between the structure and the wearer; this is perhaps the most surreal corset creation to date.

London-based Japanese designer Atsuko Kudo's corset designs are structurally more classical than those of her Japanese compatriots. Using lingerie as her focus, her designs are feminine, even lace patterned and trimmed however, her chosen material is latex rubber. Here again we see the Japanese flair for subverting and fusing the traditional with the futuristic. Her delicate designs have attracted a celebrity clientele including Lady Gaga, Grace Jones, and Beyonce, who are all looking for something which combines classic with cutting edge.

Deep plunge, pewter silk swarovski long-line corset, Velda Lauder "Gothikka" collection, 2010. Model Bex Paul.

The Modern Girl's guide to Corset Wearing

Whether you choose to wear it as underwear or as a statement piece of outerwear, wearing a corset properly is an art in itself. You will have the best experience with a corset if you choose one that fits you properly, is well finished so that you are not impaled on the boning, and one which is made from quality materials so that it will keep its shape and enhance yours. Using the correct techniques to choose, fit, lace and tighten a corset will allow the wearer to reduce their waist comfortably and safely over time. Three long-term corset wearers, Morrigan Hel, Bex Paul, and Deanne Lula Lee, reflect on how they wear a corset and what it means to them.

Corset wearing and care in the 21st century

"Tightlacing" and "corset training" are terms that are used to describe how to fit a corset correctly and comfortably to give you excellent posture and an hourglass figure. The more extreme practice of "waist training" is used to describe the process of waist measurement reduction, through the prolonged wearing and tightlacing of a corset.

To choose your correct corset size

First measure your natural waist and subtract 4 inches. For example, for a natural 28 inch waist this will give you a correct corset size of 24 inches, or the size that you will reduce your waist measurement down to with correct corset wear and practice. Measure around the narrowest part of the waist where it indents most above the hips.

For overbust corsets you will also need to be aware of your correct bust measurement and bra cup size; this is very important to achieve a perfect full-length corset fit. It's worth going to a specialist store for a bra fitting so that you know your correct cup size – most women need a smaller band size and larger cup size than they generally wear.

Lacing and fitting your corset

Open your corset, stretch out the laces at the back, so that you can comfortably wrap the corset around your body, and click the busk closed at the front. Position yourself in front of a mirror, relax and breathe deeply – you cannot hurry the fitting of a corset.

Turn sideways to the mirror so you can see your hands as you reach back and pull the two "looper laces," but not too tight. Straighten out the facing or "modesty panel" between the eyelets and laces. Stretch your arms above your head, wiggle into a comfortable position, and once more check the shape and position of the corset in the mirror.

If you are wearing an overbust corset, this is the time to rearrange your breasts into the desired position. Now, pull the laces again, always aiming for even lace lengths toward the middle, and working them back to the waist where the excess lengths will go into the loops.

How to tighten

Tighten by constantly pulling the laces from the bottom to the center, evening out the two laces, and then pulling them top to center again. Keep the two rear eyelet panels evenly spaced from top to bottom to avoid a bulging gap at the waist. Keep working top down to middle and bottom up to middle, holding taut the excess. Finally, cross the two

Woman fitting her corset

Fitting your corset and training your waist

A corset that is worn as an outer garment should be the last item you put on.

Always remember to put on your shoes beforehand, as bending will be more difficult once you are laced in.

For prolonged wear it is advisable to moisturize the skin throughly beforehand; applying a layer of talcum powder can also prolong the time that you can comfortably wear your corset and will help in absorbing perspiration and preventing chafing.

Wearing an undershirt in a natural fabric like cotton or silk is best, as the fibers allow the skin to breathe. The undershirt can be more easily washed than a corset, which will require specialist cleaning.

A corset worn as an undergarment should be worn before your final outer layer and over your underwear, stockings, and so on.

loopers holding the tension, give one last big pull, then tie the remaining lace into a bow at the center of the back of the corset.

Get used to the feel of the corset, and the natural improvement that it creates in your posture, and after 10–15 minutes the fabric will have become more pliable with your body warmth. Undo the laces a little and pull in again; the corset should be able to be laced tighter than before. This can be repeated several times to gradually reduce the space between the rear eyelet panels, allowing you to reduce the waist further. Finally the laces are knotted, usually in a double bow, so that they will not loosen by themselves. The excess laces can then be tucked under the bottom of the corset.

Eating, sleeping, and exercise

When tightlacing, always remember to relax and breathe deeply. To assist your progress it is recommended that you should drink plenty of water, eat small, regular meals of fruits, vegetables, and other fiber-rich foods. Do not eat large meals or carbonated drinks before or during corseting and avoid heavy foods. Chew food longer and take smaller bites, think "little and often."

Pilates is recommended for training the core muscles in the corset area for strength and suppleness, whilst protecting the back. Remember that firm toned bodies make tightlacing more challenging because there is less flesh to manipulate and it will take longer to relax into the corset.

For waist training, the time that you spend in the corset is much more important than the degree of tightness, so for the best results wear your corset as much as possible. If you want to reduce by more than the recommended 4 inches, you may wish to try sleeping in your corset.

Cleaning a corset

I recommend, wherever possible, using a theatrical dry cleaner to clean your corset as they will have experience in cleaning such items. If the boning is not rustproof (most modern corset boning is), it may be necessary to remove the metal boning before the corset is dry cleaned.

Sitting in a corset

Always choose the highest chair that you can, for example a bar stool or the arm of the sofa, and if you must sit on a low chair, use a cushion to elevate the hips. Corsets perfect your posture and therefore you will need to sit appropriately. There can be no slouching, no relaxed "C" shapes with the torso and pelvis; elegant strong "L" shapes work best.

Finally, always think of your corset as a work in progress. When you can close your corset completely at the back, it is time to buy the next size down and begin the slow and enjoyable process again.

Modern women and modern corsets

As part of the process of writing this book I met three inspirational modern women, all of whom have profoundly influenced the burlesque and fetish fashion scenes, and served as creative muses in the design processes of the Velda Lauder brand. We discussed the role that the corset has played in their personal and public lives and I was able to use their unique perspectives and insight to inform many of the themes explored in the book.

Morrigan Hel

Amber Erlandsson, aka Morrigan Hel, is an established model, performer, television presenter, and recording artist. With a background as a make-up artist, pole dancer, and actress, Morrigan Hel took the fetish scene by storm with her legendary and breathtaking fire performances. This in turn led to an extensive touring schedule as a featured performer with bands such Motorhead, Godhead, Hard Knox, Beyond Twilight, NFD,

Morrigan Hel on stage at KOKO London, 2006, wearing red satin and black lace "curve" corset and accessories, Velda lauder "Burlesque" collection.
© *Regis Hertrech.*

The Deathstars, H.I.M, The Murder Dolls, and Cradle of Filth. Currently, Amber is focusing her energies on her band, Nemhaim, with the release of their debut album "From the Ashes" and a European tour scheduled for 2010.

"I bought my first corset from Vollers when I was 14 years old. I must have been about 15 when I got my first corset from you [Velda Lauder], when you had your Pagan Metal shop in Soho. It took me a while to save up for it, but I was pretty determined. I've still got it to this day, although it doesn't really fit me anymore, sadly. I started going out to clubs from the age of 12, I wore a lot of make-up, backcombed my hair, and managed to get through the door regardless of my age. One of the first clubs I went to was the Electric Ballroom in Camden; my mum used to go there and a few of my school friends on the alternative scene knew about it. That then led to Slimelight, which then, of course, led on to the Torture Garden.

Dolls and film influences

"I think my She Ra dolls were to blame for my fascination with corsets! I was heavily influenced by films like *Red Sonja, Barbarella, Conan the Destroyer*, and comic book characters such as Lady Death, Vampirella and Purgatory. Basically anything with women in strong, fierce roles. Corsetry seemed to be part of their armor, but at the same time they were pulling their waists in to maintain an overtly feminine shape.

"I have never consistently worn corsets all day every day, I tried to corset train when I was around 16 or 17, but never through the night, and I only did it for a year or so. I noticed that my waist definitely changed shape and looked more nipped-in from the front. I didn't notice much sizewise though, possibly just under an inch, but it was hard to tell as your waist and stomach vary depending on the time of day and the time of the month. I don't wear corsets as much as I used to and I think saving them for special occasions keeps the excitement factor going.

"I think that as I got busier, I wore them less. I run a photographic studio and work on location, so there's a lot of hands-on work with that. I also have a band and work as a fire performer so it's really down to time and practicality. As a teenager I was constantly partying and had a lot more time on my hands. I also feel it's more rewarding to wear one for special occasions.

"I'll wear corsets for stage use, nights out, in the bedroom, and photoshoots. I work out most days now so it wouldn't be practical to wear one every day. I do still enjoy wearing them, of course, the way they look and feel. If you're into them, you're into them for life. I'd never sell any of mine even if I don't wear all of them anymore.

The benefits of a good corset

"My waist is usually 25 inches, and I can still get down to a 19 or 20 inch waist with a good corset. When I was younger and skinnier I could go to maybe 17 inches. It makes a huge difference how the corset is made as to how far you can get down. I have a Miss Katy corset and various corsets from you which were made to measure and only pull my waist in, not my ribcage. A lot of the cheaper, less well-made corsets will just crush your ribs or hip bones and hurt like hell. So the key really is going for a made-to-measure, well-made corset. Wearing it in a bit obviously helps too.

"Corsets have definitely evolved since I first started wearing them; there's a lot of great stuff out there, but they also seem to have become more mainstream at the same time. When I first started buying corsets there was no internet, so you really had to know where to go. A lot of it was word of mouth. Now all you need to do is do a search in Google! Although saying that there are also a lot more badly made corsets out there and bootlegs.

"My experience of corset wearing has been mostly very positive, although I have had boning come out and stab me in the hip bone before. That's probably my own fault for wearing it too hard and refusing to accept it's been worn out! I don't think I have any poorly made corsets anymore, I usually have them made to measure or at least make sure to buy one that fits properly from a good designer. I was wearing one to a restaurant at a fetish event and quickly discovered that eating and drinking too much champagne is not a good plan in a tightly-laced corset.

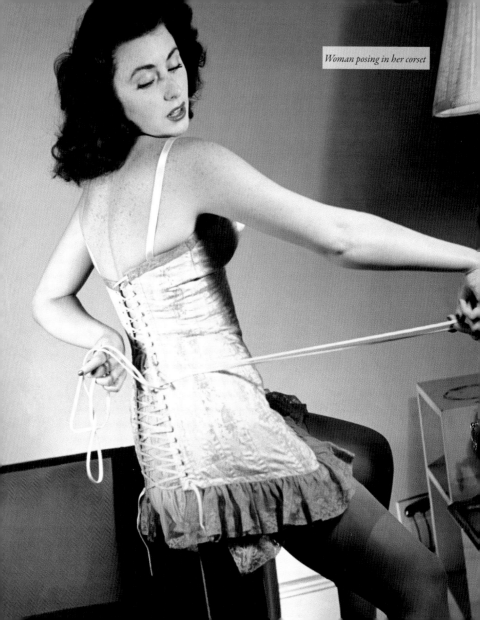

Woman posing in her corset

"I've got a few really beautiful, comfortable, and flattering corsets that I love, but I do remember trying one of those straight up and down jobs with no modesty panel that pulls in the waist, hip bones, and ribs, and then leaves you with a really unflattering "arse crack" effect at the back, not a good look. If they fit properly and feel comfortable, corsets are definitely empowering. You can lace them as tight as you want, so if you really feel like challenging yourself lace it all the way, but if you're singing or performing you'd have it laced looser, so I guess a different type of corset for every occasion. I really love real leather corsets too; they smell, look and feel amazing.

"I know there are people out there who point to corsets as a symbol of female oppression, but in this day and age, in a relatively civilized society I'd say "bollocks"! A few hundred years ago I'm sure it was a different story. Women wear corsets today because they want to, they're not forced into it, it's a choice and that in itself is empowering. I hope that corsetry will only get more decadent and more popular. I'm actually looking for a corset that would work well when singing with my band, a rock 'n roll corset range would be very cool!"

Bex Paul wearing a deep plunge, silk swarovski long line corset, Velda Lauder "Gothikka" collection, 2010.

Bex Paul

Bex Paul is a London-based burlesque performer and model. She has established herself as a firm favorite with photographers and designers alike using her unique blend of voluptuous curves, statuesque posture and cool demeanour. Bex has modeled at the London Fashion Week opening party, the Erotica Expo in London, Salon International de la Lingerie in Paris and Skin2eXpo to name a few. She is also currently in the process of setting up her own "Show Girl" accessories business.

"I first became aware of corsets when at 16 I was scouted as a model by a customer at the restaurant where I worked as a waitress; they asked me to model for one of their corset designer friends. The first time I wore a proper corset was when I modeled for you, Velda, at the Dirty Red Ball 2006, at Koko in London. I wore an amazing black-and-white outfit of a polka dot 24-inch corset matched with a striped skirt and a fabulous *My Fair Lady* style hat, and after that I was hooked. I found something which ignited a fire and excitement in my heart. I call it the "Look at me, I'm fabulous" feeling, it does wonders for a girl's self-belief.

"I bought my first corset, a black broderie anglaise curve corset, from you too. I love the look and the feeling you get from wearing a beautiful, skillfully hand crafted corset. I think the image created is one of uber femininity. For me, emphasizing one's curves is to evoke the femme-fatale within, and that in itself is extremely good for confidence, which emanates beauty.

"Since I started wearing corsets, I do wear them fairly regularly, at least once a fortnight. I adore tightlacing, and can take 8 inches off my waist comfortably, if done with a few reductions over time as the corset warms to my body. I once pulled into 18 inches with a short waist cincher, that's 10 inches off my natural waist! With more regular waist training I would easily be able to do this or more, as I have a very pliable waist. There is a certain amount of discipline required when reducing your waist dramatically. You cannot slouch, and you learn to breath slightly differently. I am usually somewhere between a 27-and 30-inch waist before I get into a corset.

Getting the waist right down

"Your [Velda's] corsets are cut in a certain way that allows my hips and ribcage to sit comfortably, with the necessary room for displacement (my body doesn't magically disappear) and ease of breathing. A series of pulls, as the corset warms over time, allows me to be pulled in quite tightly. I started by reducing my waist by only 4 inches, but now I don't feel satisfied unless I'm pulled in nice and tight by about 7 or 8 inches. I always want to be smaller, for a more dramatic effect, I want to really feel that I'm wearing a corset. Also I mainly wear loveheart shaped corsets now as opposed to the straight across ones, for an extra curvy look.

"I think that quality corsetry is still a very niche market, the key word being "quality". There are many more companies now trying to create corsets, as women seem prepared to be more experimental with fashion, but still I believe they are rarely worn other than for special occasions. I don't think real corsets will ever be "mainstream" and that's part of the draw for me; you stand out from the crowd in a great corset. I have only ever worn Velda Lauder corsets for any prolonged amount of time, and they are measured precisely to my desired fit.

"I think real steel boned corsets will always remain something of a couture fashion item, but I hope that one day soon there will be more curvy models like myself modelling them on the catwalks of fashion week events worldwide, as our curves do the corset more justice. I think corsets have something of an iconic status for those who are prepared to open their eyes and see it. Through the ages, corsets have always been there, previously perhaps seen as torturous undergarments, but currently they are seen as treasured items of curve enhancing beauty and desirable craft.

"My favorite corset experience has to be at the London Fashion Week 2010 opening party, just because I was wearing the metal silk and Swarovski-encrusted deep plunge corset that you had created specifically for me. The worst experience was trying on a corset which must have had rectangular panels, because it literally tried to crush my ribs. Sometimes I envisage myself adorned in a crystal-encrusted corset in my coffin, as a representation of when I have felt most beautiful, confident and at one with who I am.

Back detial, Velda lauder corset, 2009.

Corsets and femininity

"I believe that wearing a perfectly fitted corset allows a woman to show off and emphasize all that is female. Your posture is elevated, so you stand taller. The curvature created turns the heads of men all around the world, and they will worship your every footstep just to talk to you; because of this, for many women, there is a confidence that ensues. That said, it's females who really want to talk to you most, from super slim girls, who wish to have the form or curves which a corset can create, to much more curvaceous girls who want to dress their curves in a way that is flattering and more desirable. I think it takes seeing someone like me to give another woman the confidence to be proud of her goddessy curves and embrace them.

"I have listened to arguments about female oppression and the over sexualization of women in relation to corsetry, but I completely disagree. Never have I felt oppressed when wearing a corset, and the control is definitely in my hands. Sexualization is in the eye of the beholder, over sexualization is what people with their eyes shut imagine because they don't hold the control or the power. For me, the corset will remain a positive addition to my life. For others, I hope it allows more women to feel as perfect as they should feel, as desirable as the next, as beautiful as they are, and as strong as they need to be."

Deanne Lula Lee on stage at KOKO London, 2006, wearing Velda lauder "Burlesque Peace Warrior" collection.

Deanne Lula Lee

Deanne Lula Lee's illustrious career has encompassed jewelry, leather and hair design, modeling, marketing, PR, and fashion boutique management. Among her long list of clients she has hosted and modeled for numerous fashion magazines, TV, music videos, product launches and celebrity parties, plus London Fashion Week, Immodesty Blaize shows, Torture Garden, and the Dirty Red Ball. She has recently moved from managing Agent Provocateur in the West End of London, to a new position as manager and press contact for the Fifi Chachnil boutique in Kensington, London.

"I left the Berkshire college of Art and Design to take up a position with Jane Kahn's Kahniverous at Hyper Hyper in Kensington High Street. My style at that time was very much underwear as outerwear, bustier bra tops and corselet skirts, I was way ahead of my time! I have been corseting for 20 years, and first wore them when I started going to Goth and fetish clubs. I got seriously hooked when I was offered the part of a goth in an EMI video, *Kids of the Century* wearing a tiny borrowed waspie corset. I have never waist trained, as I am very happy with my natural hourglass shape and simply use the corset for emphasis. A well-made corset can reduce my waist from 25 inches to 18 inches in total comfort for hours. I can wear a well-made corset at work for ten hours, then change into another one to party all night, before repeating the whole process again the next day. I am very fussy with my corsets. I am a connoisseur of well-made, well-fitted beautiful corsets. I continue to wear them as I feel confident, glamorous, and comfortable. Thanks to the corset correcting my posture I have rectified the back problems I suffered from when I was younger. I love the reaction a corset receives, it's definitely a conversation starter; complete strangers will always approach to admire the shape, and to ask the size of my waist. I definitely found the best way to dress for my shape when I discovered the corset.

Hollywood inspirations

"I have a big love of old movies and the glamor of the Hollywood star. I take great pride in setting my hair and maintaining my long red finger nails and matching toes. I only ever wear seamed stockings and beautiful feminine outfits, and my corsets complete the look. I use every kind of corset, ranging from a daywear waspie in pinstripe for business meetings, to patent leather, leopard print or Swarovski crystal full-length corsets for evening wear. I have a large and very beautiful collection of corsets in many styles and fabrics to suit my mood. One time I had a patent leather curve corset stolen. I made such a fuss, letting everyone know it was a one-off and if they were ever seen wearing it everyone would know it was mine, that it was returned, pushed through my letter box the next day. I wear corsets because I feel amazing in them, I love the style, and the attention. A corset allows you to enjoy your female shape fully, and not hide your curves under baggy shapeless clothes as if you were ashamed of being curvaceous and having hips. With my heels, stockings, and corsets

I feel elegant, sophisticated, and stylish, I have always thought the reason I have been asked to host so many events is because they know I will turn up in an amazing corset! As a result I find that I am always treated like a lady, doors are opened for me, men will get up and give me their seat, and carry my suitcase; all told, my corset is empowering, never oppressing.

The importance of good lingerie

"Many lingerie companies are now designing a waspie garter belt within a range, instead of the normal suspender belt. I am very fortunate in my career to have worked with some of the best lingerie in the world. I have often been described as a "lingerie guru" and as a specialist, I understand the importance of the foundation garment to an outfit and the confidence that it gives to a woman. Your lingerie can make or break your outfit and when a woman has been fitted for a bra (not to be confused with measured) the increased confidence and posture can be seen immediately. The same applies to a corset, a badly made or fitted corset exerts pressure on the ribs and can be very uncomfortable and cause extreme distress. When I was younger I bought a cheap corset and the plastic boning came through when I was dancing, it cut into me and I had a scar for years. It is well worth spending more money on a good quality corset as an investment, I have had some of mine for 15 years and they still look amazing!'

abdominal reduction 48
Agent Provocateur 167
Alaia, Azzedine 151
Alexandra, Queen 181, 185
ancient times 28–9
animal-hide bodices 28
Anne of Denmark (1574 - 1619) 36
anthropology 102
A-POC 191
Art Deco 65

Balenciaga 164
Ballard, Bettina 145
Barron, Kay 149
beauty, suffering for 119–20
Beckham, Victoria 77, 157
belts, wasp-waisted 135
Beyonce 195
Bizarre magazine 116, 126
Blaize, Immodesty 83, 113, 114, 115
bodies 35
body consciousness 21
body modification 17, 20, 21, 137, 139
body sculpting 21, 75
body shape 11, 13, 27, 28, 32, 37, 78–9
bondage 120–1
bondage, domination and submission (BDSM) community 120
boning 13, 29, 37, 52
Boudicca (Boadicea) 13, 30, 31
Bourne, Mrs Addley 60
bras 63
bullet 70, 71, 91

bust reducing 67
cup sizes 85
long-line 73
panelled 69
soft cup 74
technological developments 73–4
breasts
display 43
flattening 35, 37
breathing 56–7, 201, 212
Brummel, Beau 47
burlesque 83, 105, 107, 109, 113, 114, 115, 165
Burns, Pete 157
bust
elevating 51, 61
flattening 35, 37
reduction 67
bust enhancement 48
bust size
increase in 98
measuring 82
bustiers 148
bustles and bustle pads 43, 51, 59
buttons 29
Byron, Lord 47

Cadolle, Herminie 84
Canadelle 74, 97
Caron, Leslie 94
Chanel, Coco 94
Chayalan, Hussein 170, 178, 180
cinema 88, 90, 91, 151
Cirque du Soleil 153
cleaning 202

Coco de Mer 167
Comme des Garçons 164
conical corsets 36, 37
contour garments 165
control 32–3
Corré, Joe 167
corselets 49
corset training 120, 137, 198, 206
Courrèges, André 98
couture 145
crinolines 51, 52
cross-dressing 121
Cunnington, P. 34
curves 69, 215, 218
Cyborg, Samppa Von 18, 19

dangers 21, 38, 41, 43, 53, 56–7
Day, Doris 94
Diary of a French Maid 128–9
Dietrich, Marlene 88
Dimanche 97
Dinka tribe, the 181, 182, 184, 185
Dior, Christian 15, 17, 83, 91–3, 94, 125, 143, 144, 145, 159, 164, 182, 185, 189
dolls 205
domination 120–1

eating 201, 207
Eden, Garden of 31–2
Edward VII, King 62
Edward VIII, King 89
18th century 40, 42, 43, 44, 45
elastic fabrics 52, 61–2, 69
Elizabeth II, Queen 89
empire line 28, 45, 46

empowerment 17, 29, 31, 33, 67
Englishwoman's Domestic Magazine, The 119–20, 121, 123
eroticism 11, 78
Eve 31–2

fashion, and female status 33
Fashion Slaves (Flower) 56–7
Fath, Jacques 143, 146, 148, 159
female body, controlling 32–3
female oppression 17
female silhouette 32, 43
femininity 215
feminist movement, the 73
fetish clubs 133, 205. see also Torture Garden, the
fetish fashions 78, 101, 121–2
fetish imagery 126, 135, 137
fetish objects 117, 119, 122–3
Finnigan, Kate 72
fitting 199, 200, 200
flapper fashions 65, 66, 67
Flower, B. O. 56–7
folklore 33
France 44, 45
Francis, Connie 71, 95
French Revolution 45
front-laced bodices 29
front-lacing corsets 47

Galliano, John 17, 143, 149, 157, 158, 159, 161, 171, 173, 180–1, 182, 185, 189
Garbo, Greta 88, 89
Gardener, Ava 68, 94

Garrod, Michael 21
Gaultier, Jean Paul 14, 76, 77, 107, 131, 143, 147, 148, 150, 151, 157, 164
Genesis, Book of 31–2
gentleman's corset, the 48, 156, 157, 161
George IV, King 47, 48
Giabiconi, Baptiste 161
Gibson, Charles Dana 59
girdles 63, 69, 74–5
Givenchy 188, 189
Glove-fitting Corsets 26
goddesses 29, 31
Golden Age of Couture: Paris and London 1947–1957, The (Wilcox) 92
Gossard 85
Gosson, Philip 34
Goth fashions 100, 102–3, 134
Grabble, Betty 88, 88
Graeco-Roman style dresses 49
Granger, Ethel 124
Great Depression, the 69, 88, 109 Greene, Alexander Plunkett 72
Greer, Germaine 99
Gypsy Rose Lee 113

Hancock, Thomas 52
Hayworth, Rita 88, 94
healthy corsets 61–2
Hel, Morrigan 203, 204, 209
Hepburn, Audrey 94
Hepburn, Katherine 89
hips 51
Hishinuma, Yoshiki 194

History of Underclothes, The (Willett and Cunnington) 34
Hollywood 69, 88–9, 91, 94, 107, 218
hourglass silhouette, the 28, 50, 51, 69

inner goddess, freeing 21
inspirations 17, 131, 171, 173, 180–1, 182
iron bodies 34

Jade, Fiona 16
Japanese traditional dress 189–90
Jeannette 22
Jones, Grace 195
Jung, Cathie 126–7

keep fit 19, 75, 201
Kelly, Grace 94
knotting 201
Koshino, Junko 171
Krafft Ebing, Richard von 122
Kudo, Atsuko 78, 193, 195
La Belle Epoque 62–3
lacing 29, 37, 199, 208, 209. see also tight lacing
Lacroix, Christian 14, 143, 148, 149, 151, 157
Lady Gaga 171, 176, 177, 195
Lagerfeld, Karl 151, 160, 161, 181
Lastex 89
latex 97
Lauder, Velda 153
Burlesque collection 112, 204, 205–7
Gothikka collection 86–7, 104,

110, 169, 196, 210
Peace Warrior collection 162, 163, 216
personal epiphany 19, 21
Salon de Tea collection 81, 111, 168
Victoria's Secret collection 179
leather 78, 209
leather bodices 13
Lebigot, Marie Rose 92
Lee, Brenda 71, 95
Lee, Deanne Lula 216, 217–19
lingerie 32, 63, 74, 173
importance of good 219
as outerwear 77
retro glamour 165, 167
long-waisted corsets 43
Louis XVI, King of France 45
low-cut gowns 43
Lycra 74, 98, 165

McCartney, Stella 77, 161, 163
McLaren, Malcolm 101, 135
McQueen, Alexander 15, 131, 143, 153, 154, 155, 164, 171, 173, 178, 180, 189
Madonna 19, 76, 77, 131
Mannikin collection 80
Marie Antoinette 44, 45
Marks & Spencer 74
meals 201
Medieval period 28, 33, 34, 35
Merry Widow corselette 93–4
Metal Couture 177
mini skirts 73, 99
Minoan snake goddess 10, 13, 31
Minogue, Kylie 150, 157

Miss Exotic World Pageant 115
Miyake, Issey 171, 174, 177, 183, 190–1, 192, 194
modern primitives, the 137, 139, 185
modern resurgence 14
Monroe, Marilyn 8, 11, 71, 91
movement, restriction of 39
Mugler, Thierry 130, 131, 143, 151, 152, 153, 155, 157, 171, 172, 173, 175, 177, 189
Musafer, Fakir 136, 137, 139, 161, 185

Ndebele, the 187
neck corsets 185, 186, 187, 188, 189, 194
New Burlesque, the 107, 109, 113, 114, 115
New Look, the 91–3, 92, 94, 125, 143, 144, 145, 164

obi, the 189–90
original sin 31–2, 33
Oswald, Judy 64
Outlaw, The (film) 90, 91
overbust corsets 198, 199

Padaung, the 185, 186, 187
Page, Bettie 105, 106
Pain, Tom 41
Papua New Guinea 184–5
Paul, Bex 210, 211–13, 215
Pearl, Mr. 21, 77, 139, 157, 159, 161
personal fantasies 121–2
petticoats, great 40, 42
Phelps Jacobs, Mary 84

physical expression 21
piercing 139
Pilates 21, 201
pin-up culture 105
Playtex 18-hour girdle 96, 96, 97–8
pleasure 127
Pleats Please 190
Poiret, Paul 64, 65
Polhemus, Ted 102
Polka-dot and Pinstripe collection 16
popularity, decline in 14
posture 48, 201, 202, 215, 218
power 17, 78, 173
pregnancy 52–3, 54–5
Presley, Elvis 95
Priestley, J. B. 63
Psychopathia Sexualis (Krafft Ebing) 122
Pugh, Gareth 153
punk fashion 101, 104, 105, 118, 119, 134, 135, 137

Quant, Mary 72, 72, 74, 98–9

rayon 85
reconstructed corsets 102
Rees, Serena 167
Regency period 45, 46, 47–9
religion 33
Renaissance 13, 21, 36
replacing 203
revival 78–9, 102–3
Reynolds, Debbie 94
Robot Couture 152, 177
Roddick, Sam 167
Rolfe, Colin 99

Rosenthal, Ida Cohen 85
rubber 78, 117, 131, 132, 133, 193
ruling classes 39
Russell, Jane 71, 90, 91

Saint Laurent, Yves 164
sales, 1920's decline 67
S-bend silhouette 58, 59
sexual revolution, the 98–9
shamanism 137
shift dresses 65, 66
shoes 45, 122, 135
side effects 19
Simpson, Wallis 89
sitting 202
Sixties, the 95–9
Skin Two magazine 133
skirts
full 145
hooped 43
mini 73, 99
wide 51
Spanx 165
Spanzelle 74
spinal distortion 56–7
sports 62
Spungen, Nancy 104
stays 48–9
stockings 67
suspender belts 67, 69, 73, 219
Swanbill corsets 60, 61, 62
sweater girl chic 91
symbolism 19
tattooing 139
technological advances 164–5
teenage trends 70, 71, 95
Teese, Dita Von 83, 105, 106,

107, 149, 157
Thompson, Lydia 109
tightlacing 78, 117, 120, 123, 125, 157, 198, 212
effects of 38, 39, 41, 53, 56–7, 124
smallest waist 124, 126–7
tactile interaction 127
tightening 29, 199, 201
tights 73, 99, 165
Torture Garden, the 117, 132, 138, 139, 140, 141, 205
Triumph 74, 85
Tucek, Marie 84
Turner, Lana 91, 93–4

under-bodices 35
underbust corsets 142, 162, 163
underwear
functions 28
medieval 34, 35
modernization 61–2
as outerwear 105, 148, 149, 167, 217
Regency period 48–9
Renaissance 37

Valentino 151
vaudeville 109, 113
Versace 151
Vicious, Sid 104
Victoria, Queen 47, 62
Victorian era 21, 51–3, 54–5, 59

waist cinching 49, 65
waist line 61

waist size 28, 51, 61, 124, 126–7, 145, 189–90, 207, 217
waist training 198, 200, 202, 212
waspie suspender belts 219
Westwood, Vivienne 14, 77, 83, 101, 105, 107, 118, 119, 135, 143, 151, 157
Wilcox, Claire 92
Wild, Judy 133
Willett, C. 34
Willie, John 126, 128–9, 131
women
discrimination 32
emancipation of 15, 63, 67
empowerment 29, 31, 33, 67
reproductive abilities 31
sexualization of 215
status 33, 51, 62, 120
subjugation 31–2
Wonderbra 74, 97, 107
Woodward, Tim 133
working classes 39
World War One 63
World War Two 69, 71, 89
Worth, Charles Frederick 145

Bizare, 1946-1969, Bizarre Publishing Company

The Corset and the Crinoline, W. B. Lord, 2008, Dover Publications inc.

The Englishwoman's Domestic Magazine, 1852-1881, publisher Samuel Beeton

Extreme Beauty: The Body Transformed, Harold Koda, 2001, Metropolitan Museum of Art

Fashion and Fetishism: Corsets, Tightlacing and other forms of Body Sculpture, David Kunzle, 2004, Sutton Publishing Ltd.

Fashion Slaves, B.O Flower, 1891, http://www.gutenburg.org/ files/22419/22419-h/22419-h.htm#article_3

Fetish Fashion Sex and Power, Valerie Steele, 1997, Oxford University Press

The Golden Age of Couture: Paris and London 1947-1957, ed. Claire Wilcox, 2007, V&A Publications.

The History of Underclothes, C. Willett and P. Cunnigton, 1951, Dover Publications inc.

Modern Primatives: Investigation of Contemporary Adornment Rituals, Vivian Vale and Andrew Juno, 1997, V/Search Publictions

Oz Magazine, ed. Richard Neville, Richard Walsh, Martin Sharp, 1963-1969, Sydney

Psychopathia Sexualis A Clinical Forensic Study, Richard Von Kraffft Ebing, 1999, Bloat Books

Skin 2

The Story of English Furniture, Bernard Price, BBC Books London, 1978

Thierry Mugler: Fashion Fetish Fantasy, Thierry Mugler and Calude Deloffre, 1998, Stoddard

Vivienne Westwood, ed. Claire Wilcox, 2005, V&A Publications

PICTURE CREDITS

Every effort has been made to contact the copyright holders for all images reproduced in this book. The Publisher apologizes in advance for any unintentional omissions or errors and will be pleased to insert the appropriate acknowledgement to any companies or individuals in any subsequent edition of the work.

Image Libraries / Companies:

Alamy: 8, 10, 12, 15, 26, 30, 40, 42, 44, 46, 64, 66, 68, 72, 76, 80, 88, 90, 182, 186

Corbis: 118, 146, 148, 158, 174, 176, 178, 182, 187, 200, 208

Getty Images: 100, 108, 114, 147, 150, 160, 166, 183, 192

Mary Evans Picture Library: 34, 36, 50, 54-55, 60, 70, 86, 88, 92, 96, 144

Bizarre Publishing company: 116, 128

Coronet Corset Company: 58

Individuals:

Bobette / Robert Doughty: 111, 168, 214

Regis Hertrich: 6, 16, 18, 19, 20, 24, 25, 81, 86-87, 104, 110, 112, 118, 132, 134, 138, 140, 169, 204, 210, 216

Rod Howe: 162

James & James: 106

Gregory Michael King: Cover

Koneko: 142

Heiko Laschitzki / Atsuko Kudo: 192,193

Ariel B Majtas: 196

Chris Moore / Alexander McQueen: 154

Chris Moore / Hussein Chayalan: 170, 178

Fakir Musafer / www.fakir.org : 136

Michael James O'Brien / Mr Pearl: 156

Ted Polhemus / PYMCA: 103

Patrice Sable / Thierry Mugler: 130, 152, 172, 175

Maria Thompson: 80

Victoria's Secret: 179

Models:

Charlet Morrigan Hel, Fiona Jade, Deanne Lula Lee, Viktoria Modesta, Bex Paul, Maz Spencer, Elaine Tang, Dita Von Teese. Laura Beduz, Chris Columbine